# YOU CAN
# CAN
# *Fly!*

# YOU CAN
# Fly!

GREG BROWN
LAUREL LIPPERT

Photos by Tom Lippert

Aviation Supplies & Academics, Inc.
Newcastle, Washington

*You Can Fly!*
by Greg Brown and Laurel Lippert
With photographs by Tom Lippert

Aviation Supplies & Academics, Inc.
7005 132nd Place SE
Newcastle, Washington 98059-3153
Email: asa@asa2fly.com
Internet: www.asa2fly.com

Published 2004 by Aviation Supplies & Academics, Inc.
Printed in Canada

07   06   05   04        9   8   7   6   5   4   3   2   1

All photography by Tom Lippert (except on p. 34—ASA photos). Cover and title page
photo: Beech Staggerwing airplane over Lake Tahoe in California
Layout design by Sandi Harner

ISBN 1-56027-543-X
**ASA-YCF**

*Library of Congress Cataloging-in-Publication Data:*
Brown, Gregory N.
    You can fly! / by Greg Brown and Laurel Lippert ; photographs by Tom Lippert.—1st ed.
        p.  cm.
        ISBN 1-56027-543-X
        1. Flight training. 2. Airplanes—Piloting. I. Lippert, Laurel Hilde. II. Title.
    TL710.B7223 2004
    629.132'52'071—dc22                    2004012255

*Dedication*

*To all those who dream of becoming pilots:*
*Congratulations on taking the first step.*
*Flying is even better than you imagined.*

# Contents

*"Do I have what it takes to learn to fly? Do I have the "right stuff"? • Some myths about learning to fly • What it really takes to be a pilot—the "real stuff"*

*Where will I learn to fly? • Who will teach me to fly? • Your first flight*

*How long will it take? • How much will it cost? • Is it better to pay for the training up front, or by the lesson? • What's the best airplane for lessons? • Does it matter what time of year I take lessons? • What equipment and supplies will I need?*

# Acknowledgments

We owe a special debt of thanks to designated pilot examiner Warren Smith whose ideas and expertise were important to the development of this book. Among the most visible of his contributions are the concepts of "Myths of flight training" and "Ten things I wish they'd told me when I learned to fly." Thanks, Warren, for your vision, support, and commitment, not only to this book, but to flight training and general aviation as a whole.

We are also grateful to our aviation friends whose photos, or those of their airplanes, appear in this book. The pleasure they show in doing what they love—flying or talking about flying—and the pride in their newly built, meticulously restored, or deeply cherished airplanes is clear.

Finally, thanks to Bert Jensen, ageless owner and restorer of red Staggerwings, for sharing his cockpit, Henry Levy for his unwavering support for all that we do, Cirrus Design for providing a new SR22-G2 for photos, Sean D. Tucker, champion airshow performer, who always gives more back to aviation than he receives, and our good friends and fellow members of EAA Chapter 1073 in Truckee, California, who will enthusiastically fly, taxi, or pose their airplanes for photos anytime day or night.

# *About the Authors*

Greg Brown, Laurel Lippert, and her husband, Tom, share a longtime passion for the freedom and adventure of general aviation flying. Like so many people, each harbored dreams of flight long before actually gaining the confidence to embark on that adventure. Once touching the controls, however, and discovering how accessible

**Greg, Laurel, and Tom**

and fulfilling it is to fly, they were hooked, as you will be too. Greg, Laurel, and Tom invite you to join aviators everywhere in experiencing the romance, adventure, sights seen, camaraderie, and amazing sense of accomplishment unique to roaming the skies.

**Greg Brown**'s love of flying is apparent to anyone who reads his *Flying Carpet* column in *AOPA Flight Training*, or his stories in *AOPA Pilot* and other magazines. A pilot since 1972, Greg was 2000 National Flight Instructor of the Year, winner of the 1999 NATA Excellence in Pilot Training award, and the first NAFI Master flight instructor. He holds an airline transport pilot certificate with Boeing 737 type rating, and flight instructor certificate with all fixed-wing aircraft ratings. Other books by Greg Brown include *Flying Carpet: The Soul of an Airplane, The Savvy Flight Instructor, The Turbine Pilot's Flight Manual,* and *Job Hunting for Pilots.*

**Laurel Lippert** began learning to fly in 1988 at age 40. Earning her private pilot certificate in midlife was a life-changing experience. A freelance writer and editor, Laurel's new passion became flying and sharing it with others. Over the next decade, she earned her commercial certificate, instrument and multi-engine ratings, and flight instructor certificate, with the "speed of a Piper Cub." She and her husband Tom fly their 1948 Cessna 170 for business and pleasure from their home airport in Truckee, California. Laurel's feature stories have appeared in *SKI, Snow Country, Sacramento,* and *Pilot Getaways* magazine where she is Editor at Large.

**Tom Lippert**'s photographic career began in 1969 as a ski photographer. He has illustrated nine books on skiing and was *SKI* magazine's instruction photographer for two decades. He illustrated a series of children's books, and his photographs are included in the Information Age exhibit at the Smithsonian's American History Museum. Tom's aerial photographs have appeared in *Pilot Getaways* magazine and illustrate *Mountain Dreamers: Visionaries of Sierra Nevada Skiing.* His aerial landscapes of the Lake Tahoe area and Sierra Nevada are displayed in Tahoe galleries and private collections.

# 1

# *Why Fly?*

Why learn to fly? The answers are simple—fun! adventure! freedom! Flying is humankind's wildest dream fulfilled—soaring among the birds, playing tag with the clouds and gazing down upon the wonders of the earth. Pilots really do get to do those things, and it's as good as it sounds. Adding to the richness is the way others look at pilots—with admiration and awe.

Can flying be practical? Of course. Flying often saves time over other forms of transportation and offers access to places not easily reached in other ways. Piloting can also make a wonderful career. But these practical benefits are not the main reasons most people initially become aviators. Rather, they are ways that pilots capitalize on the skills that bring them so much joy.

Flying light aircraft for pleasure and business may mean a trip to the Bahamas for snorkeling, or to Manitoba in wintertime to witness a total solar eclipse. Perhaps you're thinking of a flight to the Outer Banks of North Carolina or to Mackinac Island at the confluence of the Great Lakes.

Imagine soaring over the Grand Canyon at dawn and through Monument Valley at sunset, winging north to the Canadian Rockies and south to the Baja

**Flying a Super Cub over New Zealand's Southern Alps**

Peninsula. Or shaving hours off your holiday driving to visit relatives and friends while you overfly jammed freeways below. In fact, everything looks different from the air; it's freedom you can feel and a perspective like no other.

Flying is an activity for bringing families together; there are destinations where everyone wants to go, and you as a pilot hold the key to getting there. What's more, if your family features young people growing up, it's likely that some of them will catch the bug too, offering the opportunity to share adventures together even through the teenage years.

Business flying to a meeting or assignment can shorten the trip or, at the least, make it fun. For example, in a single-engine airplane, you could fly from Indianapolis to Washington, D.C., in three or four hours, or from Phoenix to San Diego in two hours. Such capability often allows you to attend meetings on short notice, then return home the same day. And nobody, other than you, will have the opportunity to lose your luggage.

You'll witness unforgettable sights seen only from the air, like the glow of snow-covered fields at night, the glory of sunset over city lights, and circular rainbows atop layers of stark white clouds. Even after years of flying, pilots still get the same big thrill every time they take off.

Among the greatest rewards of becoming a pilot are the pleasures of introducing flight to friends and family over the years, and meeting fascinating people wherever you go, some who will become business contacts or lifetime friends. Most general aviation pilots are an independent and successful lot who willingly offer a handshake and helping hand to those who share the same passion and commitment to flying.

There are indeed people who fly for a few years and stop. Usually it's because they either don't experience the joy, or they don't perceive that they have enough travel destinations. But, if you talk to such folks, you'll find that even they rarely have any regrets about having done it.

- Fly to one of thousands of airports just for fun
- Build an airplane
- Take aerial photographs
- Fly in formation with other airplane owners
- Volunteer for worthy causes like transporting sick patients
- Introduce young people to flight by giving them rides
- Do aerobatics
- Restore and fly antique airplanes
- Fly into backcountry airstrips for wilderness camping
- Fly a floatplane
- Soar in a glider

**Camping at EAA's AirVenture, Oshkosh, Wisconsin**

Flying is as challenging as you want to make it. It is great adventure and an endless source of personal growth. The more competent you become, the more confidence and self-esteem you'll gain.

Is learning to fly a realistic goal? Yes! *You can fly!* Very few people with perseverance and determination fail to achieve the goal of flight. As we all know, life's most important accomplishments are rarely free and never easy. Learning to fly *is* a big deal, and worth every penny and any hurdle.

Despite all this enthusiasm, you will probably have one disappointment upon earning your wings. No kidding, you'll be sorry that you didn't start flying sooner. So, don't wait any longer. Strap yourself in with your instructor, grab the controls, and take off!

# 2

# *Prerequisites for Flight*

*D*o I have what it takes to fly? Do I have the 'right stuff'?

Believe it or not, many of today's licensed pilots asked themselves these very questions before ever taking their first flight lesson. Let's face it, piloting an aircraft is an awesome experience, not to mention a huge responsibility. Then, on top of that, there is a certain mystique that surrounds pilots, a stereotype of superhuman courage and nerves of steel.

With all this fanfare, it's only natural that you would question your own ability. The reality, of course, is that most pilots are not the bold risktakers portrayed by Hollywood. Pilots are just normal people. They come from all backgrounds and all occupations. Somewhere out there is at least one person just like you who became a pilot.

The challenge of learning to fly will be greater for some than others. The Federal Aviation Administration, or FAA, has set minimum requirements for all phases of flight training, like knowledge test scores, and number of flight hours flying alone ("solo") and with a flight instructor sitting next to you ("dual"). However, there are many factors that can affect a person's experience.

For example, a bright, young, high school student, whose father or mother is a pilot and who has spent many hours on a computer flight simulator, might learn the feel of the controls very quickly but, due to limited life experience, may need some time to develop planning and judgment skills. A 45-year-old

professional with a family and career, on the other hand, may find that mastering the controls takes a little longer, but making decisions based on good judgment comes naturally.

The important prerequisites for learning to fly are a commitment of time and money, good health, self-discipline and self-motivation, common sense, and, ideally, the support of family and friends.

A private pilot certificate, issued by the FAA.

## Some myths about learning to fly

Aviation, by its nature, is mysterious. How can an aircraft the size of a Boeing 747 possibly fly? How do pilots figure out all those switches and dials? Unfortunately, all the mystery surrounding aviation often leads to myths and misunderstanding. Many of these myths exist because of differing requirements of being a professional pilot versus becoming a private pilot. Obviously, the requirements to qualify as a professional pilot flying for an airline are going to be more stringent than the requirements to become a private pilot flying a small aircraft that you own or rent. Let's look at some common myths that people often have about learning to fly.

### Myth #1—Only "Einsteins" can be pilots.

This is a misconception, unfortunately upheld by a few self-inflated pilots. To become a pilot, all you'll technically need is the ability to speak, read, write, and understand basic English, along with good planning skills, and the desire to learn. A high school education is more than adequate for people who want to learn to fly for personal transportation or recreational purposes. (A four-year college degree is recommended for those wishing to pursue an aviation career.)

Along the lines of the Einstein myth is the math myth. Many people believe that extraordinary math skills are required to be a pilot. Again, this is not the case. Only the basic math functions of addition, subtraction, multiplication, and division are required. Since most aviation calculations are performed with calculators, charts or graphs, advanced math skills are simply not necessary.

## Myth #2—I can't be a pilot; I wear glasses.

Not true! Don't think that just because you wear glasses or contact lenses you can't learn to fly—you can. The idea that pilots are required to have 20/20 vision grew out of World War I when pilots of open cockpit aircraft had to wear goggles. Since the goggles couldn't accommodate a pair of glasses, only individuals with at least 20/20 vision were taught to fly.

Fortunately, that's not the case anymore. Today, pilots are only required to have 20/40 vision in each eye, *with or without glasses or contacts*. As would be expected, pilots who fly professionally, such as airline pilots, are held to a slightly higher vision standard.

There are also special allowances made for individuals who are color-blind or who have use of only one eye (monocular vision). It is important to note that, while advanced surgical techniques can now be used to improve vision, some might not yet be approved by the FAA.

## Myth #3—I'm too old to learn to fly.

This common concern has long discouraged "mature" people from becoming aviators. For some reason, perhaps relating to the portrayal of young fighter pilots in novels and movies, many people believe that if they're older than 30 or 35, they don't possess the hair-trigger reflexes required to pilot a light aircraft.

This couldn't be further from the truth. Airline pilots routinely fly giant airliners all over the globe, up to age 60, then take up some other sort of flying after retirement!

# What's included in a pilot medical exam?

There are three classes of medical certificates: a first-class medical is required to fly for the airlines, second-class medical is required to fly for hire, and a third-class medical is required to pilot a general aviation aircraft.

A third-class airman medical exam is basic: eyes, ears, nose, throat, heart, lungs, plus medical and mental history. Your flight physical must be performed by a physician designated by the FAA as an aviation medical examiner. These "AMEs" can be found within range of most any active airport, even in smaller communities. (Ask your flight school for a list or check your local yellow pages directory.)

The flight physical is simply intended to determine that your general medical condition is healthy, and that you're not subject to conditions or medications that might threaten safe operations as a pilot. Very few diagnoses will keep you from getting a third-class medical certificate.

The third-class medical certificate, once issued, is valid for three years for pilots under age 40, and two years for those 40 and older. Although not required to begin lessons, you must have a third-class medical certificate before your first solo flight.

If you have questions about specific conditions or medications and how they might affect your eligibility to fly, a good place to research the subject is the Aircraft Owners and Pilots Association (AOPA) website, address shown at left.

http://www.aopa.org

If you can pass the flight physical (the same medical evaluation required for pilots of all ages), you can become a pilot. It's as simple as that. Besides, the single most important skill for success as a pilot is good judgment, which tends to develop with age, rather than physical prowess. As a result, maturity is among the most important assets a pilot can have.

### Myth #4—I'm too young to learn to fly.

There is some confusion concerning at what minimum age you can become a pilot. This often stems from news stories that pop up every few years featuring "the world's youngest pilot" flying across the country.

While these stories make great headlines, they ignore the fact that there are certain age requirements to become a licensed pilot. Simply manipulating the controls of an aircraft does not necessarily make you the pilot. The pilot is the

*"Young Eagles" learn about airplanes*

person authorized and certificated by the FAA to operate the aircraft and, therefore, is the person ultimately responsible for the safety of the flight.

There are many exciting aviation activities available for young aspiring pilots. First, some facts: you can qualify for a student pilot certificate in airplanes at age 16. This allows you to fly solo under an instructor's supervision. To become a private pilot in airplanes, allowing you to fly freely and carry passengers, you must be at least 17. There's no minimum age for starting lessons, so even if you're not

## What about flying opportunities for young people?

Now for some other neat aviation stuff you can do *right away!* First, sign up for the Experimental Aircraft Association (EAA) "Young Eagles" program at their website. You'll likely get a free airplane flight out of the deal from an airport near your home! EAA also hosts a variety of exciting scholarships, activities, and summer "Air Academies" for young people. To learn more, visit the EAA website (shown at left) or phone EAA toll-free at 1-888-322-3229. Other organizations offer camps too; for example, the National Air & Space Administration (NASA) offers summer space camps at the Kennedy Space Center in Huntsville, Alabama.

An exciting aviation organization operating in your local area is Civil Air Patrol (CAP), an official auxiliary of the U.S. Air Force. CAP does everything from flying, to volunteer work at airshows, to emergency communications, and search and rescue missions. Best of all, you can join! CAP "composite squadrons" and "cadet squadrons" accept members age 12 and up. (For "senior squadrons" you must be age 18.) For information and nearby locations, visit the CAP website.

Another fine young people's program is Aviation Explorers, affiliated with Boy Scouts of America, which accepts young men and women from ages 14 to 20. For information and to find nearby Aviation Explorer posts, visit their website.

**Young Eagles
and
EAA Air Academy
www.eaa.org**

---

**Civil Air Patrol
www.cap.gov/**

---

**Aviation Explorers
www.learning-for-
life.org/exploring/**

Did you know that you can solo in gliders at age 14? And earn your Private Pilot certificate in gliders at 16? Pretty cool, eh? We're not talking hang gliders here, but federally certificated aircraft, also called "sailplanes." Glider aircraft must meet the same FAA airworthiness and maintenance standards as other airplanes, and glider lessons are taught by certified flight instructors, just like those who teach in powered airplanes. Not only is soaring a blast, but, since gliders are "real" airplanes, the hours you log in them count towards your future flying licenses. To learn more, visit the Soaring Society of America (SSA) website at the address shown below.

**http://www.ssa.org**

old enough to earn a license yet, ask your folks to take you out to the airport and invest in your first flying lesson. Or take an "Introductory Flight" offered by nearly all flight schools. No matter what your age, you'll get to try the controls and see what it's like to fly a plane yourself! Many flight schools offer programs for young people, so call your local airports to see if any are offered.

If you have a computer, Microsoft Flight Simulator is quite realistic (especially if you use a joystick and rudder pedals with it), and not very expensive. Learn to fly any good flight simulator program well, and you'll feel pretty much at home in a real airplane when you get there. Of course flying real airplanes is far more fun than the simulator!

## Myth #5 — Women can't/don't fly.

Whoa!

Who said that? Although gender was a big issue in the early days of flying, thankfully this is no longer the case. In fact, many instructors think women make better students because they often have more patience, a gentler touch on the controls, and less ego to interfere with learning.

Although a majority of pilots are still men, more and more women are discovering they have what it takes to be private *and* professional pilots. Today, you'll see women flying themselves to business meetings, performing at air shows, acting as captains on major airlines, and teaching others to fly.

An advantage to being a female pilot today is that she will find a world of support from other women pilots, as well as a powerful camaraderie in women pilots organizations like The Ninety-Nines and Women in Aviation International.

## Myth #6 — I can't afford to learn to fly.

Learning to fly is not inexpensive — but it probably requires a smaller investment than you think. Flying can be comparable to other recreational activities such as skiing and golf, or taking a Caribbean cruise. One key benefit to taking flight lessons is that you do not have to pay all of the money up front when you start. Typically, flight lessons are provided on a pay-as-you-go basis. Therefore, the cost of the learning to fly is spread out over the length of training. That eases the burden for those on a budget.

Many young people finance their flight lessons by working at the local airport washing and fueling airplanes. Others obtain financing through loans and grants that are available for the purpose of learning to fly. Scholarships for flight lessons are often available from aviation or community organizations.

## Myth #7 — I must own an airplane to learn to fly.

Not so. Every flight school has rental aircraft available for the purpose of learning to fly. Flight time is charged by the hour only while the engine is running. The actual rental rate will vary depending upon the flight school location, and the

**Preparing for departure at Sedona, Arizona**

size and complexity of the aircraft. Some flight schools use inexpensive two-seat aircraft while others use high performance four-seat aircraft with retractable landing gear.

A compromise between renting an aircraft and buying one is to join a flying club. This often involves purchasing a fraction of one or more aircraft and sharing ownership with as many as ten people or more. The advantage, of course, is that you get to share the cost of operating and owning the aircraft with other owners, rather than carrying the burden yourself.

## What it really takes to be a pilot—the "real stuff"

Now that we have examined some of the popular myths associated with learning to fly, let's take a look at what it really takes — the "real stuff" as opposed to the "right stuff." You've taken your first flight and soared with the eagles. You can imagine yourself as a pilot and believe that the freedom of flight will be yours one day.

The truth is, the basic requirements to become a pilot, established by the FAA, are simple. Written in typical government-style language, the rules may not *seem* flexible, but some of them are. For example, hearing-impaired individuals may still become pilots but are restricted to flight operations that do not require the use of communications. A recent rule change allows certain diabetics to become pilots. Other waivers are available to individuals who can demonstrate their ability to safely pilot an aircraft. This includes paraplegics and those with limited use of extremities.

The fact is, nearly everyone has the "real stuff" it takes to be a pilot. You just have to take that first step and get started!

**Homebuilt Harmon Rocket**

**3**

# *Choosing an Instructor and Flight School*

W here will I learn to fly?
      Flight schools, instructors, and training airplanes can vary greatly, depending partly on the size and location of the airport. You may be limited to one local airport or, if you live in a metropolitan area, you may have a choice between a busier airport where airliners operate and a smaller airport with only "general aviation" aircraft (that is, non-airline, non-military).

Larger airports may have more than one flight school with many different aircraft to fly and a number of instructors to choose from. Smaller airports may not even have flight schools, but rather a few instructors, some part-time, sharing one or two airplanes for training. Each has its advantages.

A big busy airport is a cool place to take flying lessons, but it also means that you (and your airplane) will be competing with airliners and other commercial aircraft. You'll spend much of your time and money waiting for them to takeoff and land before you get your turn at the runway. However, if you learn to fly at a large airport, you will also become adept at radio communications and flying in the maze of air traffic found at major cities everywhere.

## Part 61 vs. Part 141 — *Huh?*

When shopping for flight schools, you may hear the terms "Part 61" and "Part 141." These confusing terms refer to sections of the Federal Aviation Regulations (FARs) that govern pilot training.

Part 61 defines the requirements for becoming a pilot, including the knowledge, maneuvers, and flight experience you'll need to qualify for a pilot certificate. Although the objectives are clearly defined, no particular method is described for accomplishing the required training, meaning the details are left to each individual instructor and flight school.

Part 141 offers a program option to formalize and standardize the flight training process. Flight schools operating under that section must adhere to an FAA-approved pilot training syllabus, keep more detailed records, and incorporate student progress checks.

What does all this mean to you? Not much, for most pilots. While Part 141 programs might boast of better oversight, Part 61 programs can legitimately claim more flexibility. In most cases, you as a customer would be hard-pressed to identify training differences between good programs of each type.

It's true that certain funding programs such as Veterans Administration benefits cover only Part 141 training programs. But for most aspiring pilots, flight training can be equally effective under Part 61 or Part 141.

Far more important is to select the flight school that best fits your learning style, is well run as a business, properly maintains its aircraft, and ensures that you are thoroughly trained by quality instructors.

At a smaller field, you'll have the airport and everything around it to yourself. You will learn how to watch out for other aircraft and make your own decisions about where and when to land, rather than relying on air traffic controllers to do that for you.

Whether you train at a peaceful country strip or an urban hub, your instructor will introduce you to both types of flying. Convenience is the real key to making this decision. If you have to drive far to take your lessons, you might get discouraged. Ideally, you'll choose an airport nearby that is easy to get to and conducive to learning.

## Who will teach me to fly?

The single most important factor when starting your lessons is lining up the right flight instructor (sometimes called CFI for Certificated Flight Instructor). Since flying is largely taught one-on-one, the right instructor will greatly enhance your quality of learning, your safety and competence, and your ultimate enjoyment of flying.

Start by asking any acquaintances who fly locally if they can recommend a good instructor or flight program. The next step is to go to nearby airports, visit several different flight schools, if possible, and interview a number of flight instructors at each. Check each school's references by talking to some recent graduates, just as you would with any other professional service. You're about to make a significant investment in yourself, and you don't want any surprises.

For most people, there are a few rough spots during the first ten or fifteen lessons. That's when a good instructor, whom you relate to well, makes all the difference. To evaluate each instructor you interview, ask him or her to explain the process for earning your Private Pilot certificate. Take time to learn something of his or her instructing philosophy. You might also ask a question, such as, "Can you tell me what makes an airplane turn?" or "What, exactly, is a stall?" that will give you a sense of how the instructor explains a complex idea.

Along with being knowledgeable, your instructor should be patient, calm, and thorough, someone who listens well to you, explains things clearly, and has a relaxed sense of humor. You're going to spend many hours together in close quarters, so you'll learn faster if you respect and like this person.

You might think that more experienced instructors are better. But, it isn't necessarily so. Your instructor has completed a very intensive course of training, wrapped up by an extremely challenging one-on-one test, to FAA standards. If your flight instructor communicates well, and demonstrates professionalism and good teaching skills, don't be too concerned if he or she hasn't been at it for long. Many new instructors are really sharp. Sure, they may have less experience than some of the old-timers, but what they do have is fresh knowledge and enthusiasm.

Many flight schools use "stage checks" where several times during your training you'll fly with an experienced instructor whose job it is to make sure your training is going well. (Usually the first stage check is either just before or just after your first solo flight.) Stage checks provide the opportunity for you to get a second opinion, which is good for everybody.

Finally, each teacher-student relationship is unique, and, although there are certain procedures to follow and standards to achieve, every instructor has a

**Flying a Beech Staggerwing over Lake Tahoe**

slightly different way of sharing what he or she knows. Keep in mind that you can learn something from everyone, and the more knowledge and experiences you seek, the better pilot you will become.

Once you've found what appears to be a good instructor and flight school, make an appointment immediately and get started with the flying! Understand that you can change instructors or flight schools relatively easily if the need arises, though it's best to keep the number of such changes to a minimum to save time and money.

## Your first flight

Your first flight will be thrilling—all those beliefs you had about life being ruled by gravity will fly out the window. You will quickly realize that flying is exactly what you should be doing, and you can't imagine not going up again—soon.

To schedule your introductory flight or first flying lesson, contact a flight school or a business on the airport that offers airplanes for rent and instructors for hire. (Look in the Yellow Pages under "Aircraft Flight Training Schools" or "Aircraft Schools.")

Your instructor will likely begin the lesson by showing you how to "preflight," in other words, make an exterior examination of the airplane before flight that will include checking oil and gas levels, tire pressure, and free movement of the control surfaces.

When you climb into the airplane, you'll be sitting in the left seat—the pilot's seat! From the very first lesson, you are no longer just a passenger or observer. The instructor will explain a few of the basics, like flight controls and the primary

There are some questions you might want to ask before getting into the airplane for your first lesson, such as, "Where are we going?" If there is something you'd like to see from the air, like your house, a nearby city, or a local lake, now is the time to suggest it. And, "What will we be doing?" The instructor should outline what he or she has in mind, based on the amount of time you've scheduled for the airplane. If you've scheduled an introductory flight, sometimes called a "discovery flight," you may only get a bargain-priced 20-minute flight that gets you up in the air, but not much else. A true "first lesson," which we recommend, often means a full hour of flying time during which you'll really learn something.

It's also a good idea before the flight to tell your instructor why you're interested in learning to fly, and what sorts of missions you have in mind upon becoming a private pilot. That way he or she can tailor the experience to help address your specific needs and desires.

Finally, "Will you have time to talk with me after the flight?" Ask your instructor to allocate enough time afterwards to discuss both the flight itself and details of setting up a flight training program. You're going to enjoy this, so be prepared to schedule your next lesson before leaving.

Make sure this flight gets documented in a logbook! This little book will be with you throughout your training—and beyond—and your first flight is a great time to get your logbook started.

The Standard PILOT MASTER LOG
ASA-SP-6

instruments. All trainer aircraft are equipped with "dual controls," meaning both you and your instructor will have a complete set.

At the instructor's direction, you will learn how to use the rudder pedals to steer the airplane toward the runway. After years of driving cars, it's common for new students to want to steer the airplane using the control wheel, which won't work. In fact, the instructor may ask you to put your hands in your lap to break the habit.

Depending on factors like weather, airplane traffic, and your confidence level, the instructor will let you fly the airplane, or at least "follow through" on the controls by resting your hands on the control wheel and feet on the rudder pedals. By moving the control wheel left and right, forward and back, and applying foot pressure to the rudder pedals, you will make gentle turns, gradual climbs and descents.

If, by chance, some aspect of your first flight experience is not great, don't be discouraged. Consider it an experience by which to measure the next one, and, if necessary, try another instructor or flight school or airport. It's not your fault; it's just one of those things that happens.

Don't expect to understand everything on your first flight. Initially, the noise may be unsettling, and all those switches and dials may be a distraction to the sensation of flying. Chatter from the radio will likely sound like gibberish. But when you start taking lessons, the pieces of the puzzle will soon begin to fit into place. You will have experienced one of the most exhilarating sensations in the world, the thrill of flight. It will stir your emotions and generate excitement beyond your wildest dreams.

# 4

# *Getting Started*

*H*ow long will it take to become a pilot?

This question is not as simple as it sounds. There are a great many variables in learning to fly because each student pilot is an individual and learns at a different rate. If you're a fast learner and the conditions are right—that is, the weather is consistently good enough for flying, an instructor is available, and you have the time to study and practice—it's feasible to earn your license within a few months.

Occasionally, circumstances draw out the process, however. If you live in the mountains, for example, you may need more hours learning about the challenges of flying where the air is thinner and the weather less predictable. Or personal concerns, such as work or family, might interrupt your progress.

While some situations cannot be anticipated, others may be within your control. If you stretch out your training through infrequent lessons, you may spend almost as much time reviewing previous lessons as learning new ones. The bottom line is, the more often you can fly, the better. Most instructors recommend that student pilots schedule a minimum of two lessons per week. Of course, more than that is great, but two lessons seem to be just enough so you retain what you've learned from one lesson to the next. As with other cumulative learning activities like tennis or golf, if your lessons are spread out too much, it's easy to lose the "feel" from one session to the next. Flying less than once a week will almost certainly slow the process, because a good deal of every lesson will be consumed in "catching up" from the last one.

Individual flight lessons normally begin with a "preflight briefing" from the instructor, or a synopsis of what you will be working on before you get into the air. Then you'll fly together, usually for around an hour; you'll be surprised at how quickly your brain gets saturated, especially early in your training (which is why most lessons won't exceed one hour). After the lesson, you and your instructor will review your flight, giving you an opportunity to ask any questions that came up (a "postflight briefing"). Based on two lessons per week, expect four to six months to earn your pilot's license. Obviously, the more you fly, the quicker you'll be ready to take your final test (the "checkride").

## What can I do with a Private Pilot certificate?

Your first flying objective will be to earn your "Private Pilot certificate." (Although many people call it a "Private Pilot license," it is officially a certificate.) As a private pilot you'll be licensed to fly single-engine airplanes in good weather, with passengers, anywhere you want to go for pleasure or personal business. Imagine that—an airplane key in your pocket, and all those places to fly!

Few people actually earn their certificates in the official minimum of 40 hours of flight training. Fifty to 55 hours is a more realistic target, and many people take longer than that, especially if they fly infrequently. Most instructors agree that the more training you get as a student, the more confident you will feel when you leave the nest. So, more hours of training is not a bad thing, providing you continue to progress. The additional experience can only give you a broader foundation for your future flying.

## How much will it cost?

A range of factors will determine your total investment in flight training. First of all, flight school costs vary based on location, overhead costs, and the capital invested in aircraft and facilities. An outfit flying new airplanes, working out of a beautiful building in an urban area, must charge more than one that is operating older airplanes out of a rural airport.

Next, there's the issue of government minimums required to earn a pilot certificate, versus the practical realities of learning all you should know to operate proficiently as a pilot. Technically, one can earn a Private Pilot certificate in as little as 40 flight hours, but as mentioned earlier, it will likely take a bit longer than that.

When you visit flight schools and ask them to detail costs, most show costs based on the minimums, because that is what their competitors do. So, ask each flight school or instructor you interview to be totally honest about what it's *realistically* going to cost.

"I see from your Private Pilot information sheet that it's possible to earn a pilot certificate in 40 hours, but I understand that's not realistic for most people.

### How much should I budget for flight training?

Your flight school will help you determine the minimum investment required to earn your pilot's license, based on federal requirements and local aircraft rental and instructional rates. Few pilots actually complete their training in the minimum possible time and budget, however. Of course, there are no guarantees as to exactly how long it will take for any particular individual to master flying a plane, but this realistic budget worksheet should give you a better idea of how much to realistically budget for the process, assuming you diligently prepare for each lesson and fly regularly.

| Realistic Private Pilot Training Budget Worksheet | | |
|---|---|---|
| Aircraft rental: | 50 hours x $____ per hour | $ |
| Flight instructor: | 40 hours x $____ per hour | $ |
| Ground school classroom/self-study materials | | $ |
| CFI ground instruction: 20 hours x $____ per hour (by your flight instructor, in addition to ground school) | | $ |
| Reference books, including private pilot manual, study guides, FAR/AIM, aeronautical charts, flight guide, and flight computer | | |
| Computerized Knowledge Test fee | | $ |
| Pilot Examiner's Practical Test fee | | $ |
| **Total estimated pilot training budget** | | $ |
| | | $ |

## How does airplane rental work?

Probably, when perusing prices down at the flight school, you've wondered how airplane rental actually works. The first and most important thing to understand is that, when renting an airplane, you pay a fixed hourly rate based only on the time the engine is running. That normally includes all costs associated with the operation of the aircraft, including fuel, oil, insurance, maintenance, and a profit for the flight school. (This is known as a "wet" rate. A few flight schools charge less for the plane but require renters to pay for gasoline separately; that's known as a "dry rate.")

The significance of this pricing structure is that if you rent a plane and fly somewhere for a day, you don't pay the rental rate while the airplane is parked. Sounds more affordable that way, doesn't it? The one exception is that, since businesses can't afford to have you fly their airplane fifteen miles away and park it there for a week, most outfits have a daily minimum for non-training flights. Even this is usually negotiable, however, if you make your flying needs known ahead of time.

Based on your experience here at the flight school, how much should I budget to earn my Private Pilot certificate?" At that, the instructor will breathe a sigh of relief and give you a more accurate target. (We recommend that you budget for 50 to 60 hours, then work diligently to come in close to that.)

By now you should be realizing that you can personally impact the size of your training investment. A great deal of the cost boils down to the motivation and availability of each individual student. Of course, there can be factors outside of your control, like weather. But, if you prepare well for each lesson and fly regularly, you are much more likely to achieve the lower end of that range.

Comparing the cost to other forms of recreation, learning to fly is quite affordable for something that offers a lifetime of pleasure. And, even though one day you may choose not to fly, you will *still* be a pilot. You may not be current, but since pilot certificates do not expire, you will *always* be a pilot, as long as you live. That's worth a lot.

### Is it better to pay for the training up front, or by the lesson?

Many flight schools offer the choice of paying in advance or paying by the lesson. Each has its advantages.

Those on a budget often benefit from paying by the lesson as it allows you to get started while the urge is hot, rather than waiting in order to come up with a lump sum. While the flight school may offer a discount if you pay in advance, do so only if you're confident of its reputation and don't anticipate switching flight schools at some point. Occasionally, flight schools, like other businesses, cease operations, taking customer deposits with them. So, if you do decide to prepay for your training, be sure to check references and satisfy yourself that the company is financially stable.

## What's the best airplane for lessons?

Most people learn to fly in single-engine "trainer" airplanes. Any number of different aircraft models would be excellent for learning to fly, so the decision generally boils down to your budget and what's available at your local airport.

Despite differences in appearance and the fact that some airplanes have the wing on top while others have it on the bottom, and some airplanes have doors

1939 Beach Staggerwing biplane

Cessna 195 with radial engine

with hinges on top instead of on the side, most training planes handle pretty similarly. After earning your pilot certificate, you'll be able to "check out" in different models than you learned in. In most cases, that will require only an additional hour or two with your instructor.

So, pick the airplane that looks most exciting to you and fits your price range, and go for it! If money is tight, you can always learn to fly in one of the more economical models. Then, when you finish, check out in something more glamorous so you can impress your friends on their first flight with you as pilot!

Rutan-design Vari-Eze with canard wing and pusher

2004 all-composite Cirrus SR22-G2

## What's a checkout?

An aircraft "checkout" with a flight instructor is an opportunity for a licensed pilot to become familiar with a different make or model of airplane, other than the one he or she is accustomed to flying. Within the same "class" of aircraft (single-engine, for example), airplanes can have variations in systems, performance, and limitations. Aircraft rental businesses require pilots to be "checked-out" in a make or model of airplane by flying with an on-staff instructor who can introduce them to its differences.

## Does it matter what time of year I take lessons?

When it comes to flying, there's no time like the present. It is true that, depending on your location, winter may mean missing a few lessons due to bad weather. But, at the same time, you'll get the opportunity to really learn about making weather decisions with your flight instructor there to help you.

Winter days offer some of the best flying weather, because colder air is generally clearer and calmer. In the summer, it's usually better to fly early in the morning before the air heats up and creates turbulence and haze, or late in the day when it cools down. As you become more proficient, you'll want to fly with

### What if I'm uncomfortable with turbulence?

Although getting comfortable with turbulence is sometimes an adjustment for new pilots, any real fear goes away with experience. That's because you'll soon learn that turbulence rarely poses any danger to a properly trained pilot. What's more, after flying awhile, turbulence becomes surprisingly predictable for pilots.

Wind

your instructor in many different kinds of weather to understand how it affects your airplane and to learn how to react.

So, whatever the time of year, get started right away and make seasonal weather decisions part of your learning experience.

## What equipment and supplies will I need?

Soon after you begin your training, you will need to invest in Private Pilot training materials, written and flight test guides, and FAA pilot regulations.

Bumps can often be seen coming just as clearly as ruts ahead when driving a gravel road. And like bumps on a gravel road, when turbulence can be anticipated ahead of time, it generally ceases to be disturbing.

Most turbulence at the altitudes where light planes fly comes from just two sources: uneven heating of the ground and flow of wind over terrain.

The intensity of turbulence depends upon temperature, wind velocity, weather, and terrain. It can range from the occasional gentle bump to a consistent roller-coaster ride. Of course, a few manifestations of turbulence do indeed pose hazards, like when associated with thunderstorms or powerful mountain winds. Those situations we lightplane pilots are trained to avoid.

The knowledge of how turbulence is formed can often be used to our advantage. For example, while avoiding downdrafts in mountainous terrain, savvy pilots can capitalize on updrafts to gain altitude by understanding where they form.

(These are available in the form of books, videos, or CDs.) Before you take any cross-country flights, you will also need a plotter, a flight computer, one or two aeronautical charts, and an airport facility directory. Usually, these items can be purchased in a kit, which is less costly than buying them individually. As there are many different choices for

**You will have many choices for ground school materials.**

materials, your instructor will probably recommend specific ones she or he likes to use. Most are sold at pilot shops or right there at the flight school. You can also buy them online through a number of different aviation suppliers.

Once you get rolling on your training and know you're going to stick with it, plan to invest in a personal headset. If your budget allows, you may want to consider one of the new "active noise-canceling" models. (A number of companies make these, and most offer factory service where they will fix problems at no charge, for the life of the headset.) A headset will make your flying experience more pleasant as, without one, ambient noise in most small airplanes is loud and distracting, and can over time be harmful to your hearing.

After earning your Private Pilot certificate, there's no shortage of great aviator goodies to put on your list for holidays and birthdays. For example, one popular accessory is a portable GPS (Global Positioning System) unit, an extremely useful navigation aid that is not installed in all airplanes.

# 5

# *Your Flight Training*

## What to expect

Any good flight instructor will have a syllabus, or outline, for your flight training that he or she will share with you. In general, your Private Pilot training sequence will go something like this.

For the first seven to 12 hours of flight time, you will develop the basic skills of controlling an aircraft: climbing and descending, making precise turns, both shallow and steep, flying the plane slow and fast, learning to control the plane by reference to instruments and the ground, and acquiring skills to avoid and recover from stalls.

At the same time, you will begin acclimating to the flying environment, including operating the radio, acquiring weather information and analyzing its effects, learning the flow of traffic and about collision-avoidance techniques, and finding your way around the local geographic area.

Once you've gotten the mechanics of flying the plane pretty well down, you'll work on mastering takeoffs and landings, with an eye toward preparing for solo flight. Landings are fun, but they're challenging. Be prepared to complete

## What are these "stalls" I keep hearing about?

If there's a single most misunderstood word between pilots and non-pilots, it must be the word "stall." Until becoming a pilot, every automobile driver knows unequivocally what that word means—the engine quit.

When pilots talk about stalls, however, they're not referring to the engine stopping. The stalls you will practice as a pilot are "aerodynamic" stalls; that is, certain maneuvers create a separation of airflow over the wing causing it to lose lift.

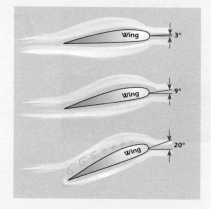

Have you ever noticed how sometimes when launching a paper airplane, the nose points too high up into the air, and the plane comes to a stop and dips toward the ground? In pilot terms, that's a stall. Stalls occur when a wing's "angle of attack" becomes too great, and it ceases to fly. That's true whether the engine is running or not.

How do you "unstall" a wing? It's simple—return smooth airflow over the wing by lowering the nose of the plane. (Adding power is often part of the recovery procedure.) If that sounds simple, it is. Practicing stalls is required of every student pilot; the goals are simply to learn what stalls are, how to avoid unintentional stalls, and how to recover when they do occur. Take time to understand the principles ahead of time on the ground, and you'll find practicing them to be interesting and fun, particularly once you get the hang of them.

four to five lessons or more in the traffic pattern before you start feeling comfortable with touchdowns.

When you and your instructor feel you're ready, you'll be signed off by your instructor for one of the most exciting events of any pilot's flying career, your first solo. Normally, the first solo is simply three takeoffs and landings in the traffic pattern. That may not sound like much, but, rest assured, you'll have trouble keeping your feet on the ground for several weeks afterward knowing that you successfully flew an airplane by yourself!

Final approach to Runway 28 at Truckee, California

## What is a "traffic pattern"?

Almost everyone has heard of airport traffic patterns, but until they become pilots few know what they are. Years ago it was recognized that, without some sort of consistent arrival and departure procedures, the risk of collisions at airports was significant, especially at airports without operating control towers. What evolved was a standard airport traffic pattern formed as a rectangle around the runway in use.

"Legs" of the traffic pattern include flying downwind (parallel to the runway), then base (a turn across the wind) and final (a turn upwind, toward the runway). Unless otherwise directed by a control tower or published exception, all turns in a standard traffic pattern are made to the left. At airports without an operating control tower, pilots are encouraged to report their position by radio on every leg, so as to inform others flying in the area.

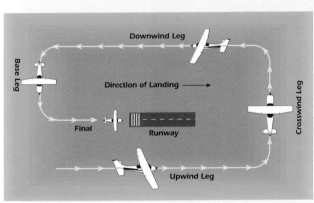

## How do pilots know which runway to land on?

Finding the runway specified by the control tower for landing is surprisingly easy, because runway numbers are selected to match the plane's compass heading on landing. Simply take the compass heading and delete one zero to find the runway number. For example, a pilot approaching Runway 27 would be landing in a westerly direction, and therefore would see 270° displayed on the magnetic compass.

Approaching that same runway from the opposite direction, however, you would see "9" painted on the runway, and 090° on your compass. That's right, there's a different number on each end of a runway. (The overall runway in this example would be known as "Runway 27/9.")

In most cases, the runway is selected to allow the pilot to land most directly into the wind since pilots always want to land into the wind, if

Compass

possible. So, if the wind is blowing from the west in this example, the pilot will want to land on Runway 27. If it's from the east, Runway 9 is preferable. And, if the wind is from the south? Runway 18 would be preferred, if there is one; otherwise, the pilot will need to make a "crosswind landing."

Next comes a period of refining your flying skills, a mixture of solo flight and dual lessons with your instructor, including an introduction to new skills such as flying at night. From there, it's on to cross-country flying. You and your instructor will make several cross-country training flights, both day and night, to develop the skills for navigating an airplane to destinations away from your home airport. Then, you'll be signed off for more great adventures, flying an airplane by yourself from your home airport to distant destinations on solo cross-country trips.

Those requirements completed, you'll spend the remaining training hours brushing up for the big day—your Private Pilot practical test (or checkride) where you'll demonstrate, through an oral exam and flying the plane, the piloting skills and knowledge that will allow you to be certificated as a pilot and carry passengers.

## What is a cross-country flight?

"Cross-country" means a flight to an airport other than the one the pilot took off from. A cross-country flight can be a short or long distance, but it requires some form of navigation, and perhaps one or more stops before reaching a destination airport. A certain amount of cross-country flying will be required to qualify for your Private Pilot certificate. Your solo cross-country flights as a student pilot must be at least 25 miles long. These will be among your most memorable flights, because, for the first time, you will have the pleasure of flying yourself alone from one place to another.

## The FAA tests

When you first begin your flying lessons, you probably won't be thinking much about the FAA pilot examinations. You'll be too busy working hard and just having fun. Your instructor, by contrast, is aware that, not only are the lessons designed to teach you the skills to fly safely, but they are also preparing you to pass the FAA tests.

Besides flying the minimum number of hours required to apply for the Private Pilot certificate, you must also prepare to take the FAA's computerized knowledge test, plus an oral test and a flight test. Getting ready to take each of them requires commitment by you and also your instructor who knows ahead of time what you will be tested on.

### Aeronautical knowledge and the computerized test

Ground training is an essential part of learning to fly. Some of the areas you will study and be tested on are federal regulations, aerodynamics, use of aviation charts, radio communication procedures, aviation weather, weight and balance computations, airplane systems, and, most importantly, good judgment and decision making.

The "Knowledge Test," formerly known as the "written" exam, is now computerized and given by an authorized testing center. It can be taken at any time during your training, but must be successfully completed before taking the "Practical Test," or flight test. The knowledge test consists of 60 multiple-choice questions. The questions and answers are published, so you can get a good handle on them before taking the test. A grade of 70 percent or better is required to pass, and you can retake it if you fail.

You have numerous options for completing "ground school" in preparation for the knowledge test. If you have the opportunity to take a good classroom course, you'll have the benefit of someone to explain things in detail. The flight school where you'll take your flying lessons may offer one on the premises. Classroom ground schools can vary in quality from terrific to worthless, so if considering that route, be sure to contact past attendees for references on the course and teacher. Some community colleges offer Private Pilot ground school courses, too.

Self-study is another option, if you have the temperament for it. Along with a number of books that can be used for home study, audio and video tapes, and DVDs are popular. The latest computer-based training courses integrate preparation for both the knowledge test and your individual flight lessons. They are interactive, effective, and fun.

If after home study you feel you need more, you can always sign up for an accelerated "weekend ground school" before taking the knowledge test. Although a weekend is mighty short for learning all there is to know about flying, the combination of home study followed by a weekend ground school usually works

## What flight experience will I need to become a private pilot?

The FAA requires a minimum of 40 hours of flight training be logged in a single-engine airplane for the Private Pilot certificate. That training must include:

✈ at least 20 hours of dual flight training with an instructor, incorporating
  • 3 hours of cross-country flight training
  • 3 hours of night flight training
  • 3 hours of flight training by reference to instruments only
  • 3 hours of flight training in preparation for the practical test
✈ and at least 10 hours of solo flight training, including
  • 5 hours of solo cross-country time
  • 1 solo flight of at least 150 miles total distance
  • 3 takeoffs and landings at an airport with an operating control tower

Of course, in actuality, you'll probably need more than the minimums to master each of the above skills, but this at least gives you an idea of what's required.

well. You get in-depth information through the reading material, and then the weekend ground school makes for a great review of what you've learned.

You can either go ahead and start the ground school before beginning flying lessons, or wait until you start flying to do it. In any case, don't feel you must complete the ground training before flying. Once you've spent a little time in the cockpit, much of the ground school knowledge makes a lot more sense. However, it would be wise (and your instructor may require it) to complete your knowledge test before you begin your cross-country training.

The results of the Private Pilot knowledge test are good for two years, so, as long as you feel that you can complete the flying lessons and take the flight test within two years, you can complete your ground school studies anytime.

## Flight proficiency and the practical test

The FAA requires that you receive training in specific "areas of operation" to become a pilot. Your knowledge of this material will be tested in a practical test, also known as a "flight test" or "checkride." The list may look overwhelming, but actually you'll be practicing one or more of these every time you take a lesson.

- preflight preparation and procedures
- airport operations
- takeoffs, landings, and go-arounds
- performance and ground reference maneuvers
- navigation
- slow flight and stalls
- basic instrument maneuvers
- emergency operations
- night operations
- postflight procedures

How do you know when you're ready for the flight test? Well, your instructor, who's been flying with you and guiding you through the learning process, will help make that decision. You will have invested 40, 50, or more hours together in the cockpit learning and polishing your new piloting skills. You will also have spent quite a few hours flying by yourself, under your instructor's guidance, perfecting all aspects of flying.

The Private Pilot practical test consists of two parts: an oral examination and a flight test in the airplane. All the items you will be tested on are clearly outlined in a small FAA book called *Private Pilot Airplane Practical Test Standards*, or "the PTS" as it's often called.

It's common for student pilots to compare their training progress with someone else's. ("I've logged 50 hours and I'm *still* not ready to take the test!") But those rare pilots who complete the training in the minimum 40 hours are not necessarily better than those who take longer. In fact, many pilots who

exceed the minimum training time before taking the test are more confident than the fast learners. Although there may be minimum numbers of hours required for elements of your flight training, there is no *maximum* number of hours for anything. If you feel you need it and have the time and money, you can practice, practice, practice before you take the flight test.

## 6

# *Making the Most of Your Flight Training*

## *B*e prepared

How fast and how well you learn is up to you. By preparing thoroughly for each flight or ground lesson *before* meeting with your instructor, you will increase your understanding of the material and ability to assimilate it. There will still be questions to ask before or after the lesson, but there is a greater chance of grasping the answer if it sounds familiar.

Conversely, if you don't prepare, you waste your money and your instructor's time, even though he or she will still get paid. Flight instructors love students who come to their lessons prepared (by reading, watching a video or DVD, or using computer software) and are eager to apply what they've studied to their experience in the air or on the ground. Here's how to save time and money.

## Quiz your instructor

It's in your best interest as a flight student to examine at *every lesson* where you are in your training syllabus, how you're doing, and what will happen next.

1. Flying lessons are supposed to be fun!

2. Other student pilots are great support. Seek them out.

3. Learning plateaus are normal.

4. Second opinions are very valuable.

5. Consistent scheduling is critical; commitment is required.

6. You don't have to be a math expert or exceptionally smart.

7. The pilot tests are not that big of a deal when you're prepared.

8. It's not just flying; you have to study, too.

9. Not all flight schools and flight instructors are created equal.

10. While extremely challenging, learning to fly is more rewarding than you ever dreamed.

Flight students are singularly unqualified to judge their own flight training progress, never having done anything like it before. So, the only way to keep a handle on your progress is to understand the details of your training program, step by step, and monitor at all times where you are and where you're headed.

The most important objective is to always understand what remains to be accomplished for you to complete your pilot certificate. Many flight students, about halfway through primary training, begin to seriously wonder whether they will ever get finished. But, if they're clear on what remains to be addressed, the end goal stays in sight.

Querying your instructor about upcoming training challenges is equally important. When a student pilot knows what's going to happen ahead of time, he can put up with a heck of a lot more difficulty than if he hasn't been briefed.

Therefore, at the end of every lesson, ask your instructor to summarize your progress relative to the syllabus to show you where you need improvement and how that will be accomplished, and let you know where you excel. Pilots-in-

training tend to notice only what they did wrong on a given flight, so it's important to recognize after every lesson the many things you are doing well.

## Remember, you don't have to be brilliant

There's a popular aviation saying that "a good pilot is always learning." One reason is that there's so much to learn! Any experienced pilot worth her wings will tell you she still learns new things all the time. That's part of the fun of being a pilot.

Fortunately, you needn't know "everything" to pass the Private Pilot knowledge and flight tests. People sometimes delay their tests unnecessarily because they unrealistically want to have total command of all the knowledge and skills in the aviation universe before being tested.

Student pilots are in the tough spot of having nothing to compare their performance against. Therefore, they tend to assume that challenges they face are unique to themselves. That's why it's important to factor in the advice of your flight instructor regarding when you're ready to take the tests. He or she flies with many students and, thus, has a perspective on how you're doing.

As long-time instructors, we can assure you that *every* pilot adding to his or her skills faces these challenges. So, don't get discouraged, and keep plugging away. You'll be glad you did! Flying is still the same kick for us today as it was back when we started. And you're going to feel the same way!

## Build a support and learning network

Since learning to fly is a challenging endeavor, it's valuable to get to know some fellow flight students for sharing of insights on everything from stalls to checkrides. Encouragement is another benefit. Learning that other pilots find the same maneuvers difficult always seems to help prevent frustration at the rough spots.

It also helps to become part of the aviation community. Join pilot associations like EAA (Experimental Aircraft Association) and AOPA (Aircraft Owners and

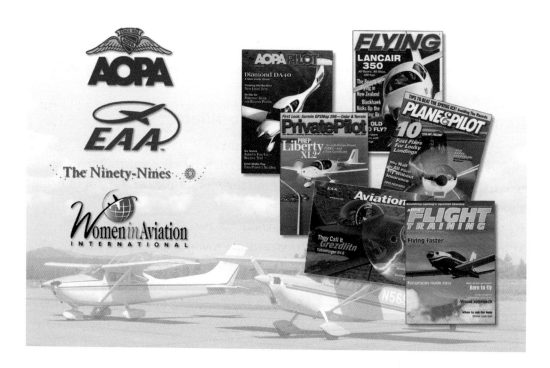

**Biplanes taxiing for takeoff**

Pilots Association). The Ninety-Nines and Women in Aviation International are excellent women pilots' organizations with local chapters at even the smallest airports.

Subscribe to some good general aviation publications like *Flying, AOPA Pilot, Private Pilot, Plane and Pilot, Sport Aviation*, and *Pilot Getaways. AOPA Flight Training* is a particularly good magazine for new pilots; not only does it specifically address student pilot topics, but your instructor can issue free subscriptions.

**http://flighttraining.aopa.org**

There's a great deal of learning to be derived from such magazines, well beyond your lessons, and they will increase your familiarity with aircraft and aviation issues. Among the most valuable benefits is learning about pilot errors and incidents you hope never to encounter yourself; you can effectively become a safer pilot by reading about someone else's mistakes. Those same publications also highlight exciting things to do with that soon-to-be-held pilot certificate, including flying different types of aircraft and visiting interesting destinations by airplane.

"Hangar flying," or listening and telling stories about personal flying experiences, is undoubtedly one of the best ways to learn about flying. If you have time to linger at the airport coffee shop or one of the open hangars, you'll get to know some seasoned pilots, many of whom gladly share their flying experiences. They know that every pilot has made his or her own mistakes and can learn from others, if only the stories are told.

## Expect learning plateaus

Every pilot runs into an obstacle or two during training, excelling at some lessons while becoming frustrated with others. This should in itself be no surprise to you, but since few student pilots hear about the challenges of their peers, they sometimes assume that only they find certain maneuvers or concepts difficult.

If you quiz your instructor, you will learn that every student at the airport

### What if I find parts of training difficult?

Every pilot-in-training experiences occasional challenges in mastering flight. These "learning plateaus" are entirely normal, and in fact are so common that they're illustrated in every instructor's professional reference, the *Aviation Instructor's Handbook*.

To quote from that book, "...in learning motor skills, a leveling-off process, or a plateau, is normal, and can be expected after an initial period of rapid improvement. The instructor should prepare the student for this situation to avert discouragement. If the student is aware of this learning platform, frustration may be lessened."

The point here is that, if you find pilot training difficult at times, don't get discouraged—it happens to everybody. Your instructor will help you overcome learning plateaus as you encounter them; they are a normal part of training.

experiences hurdles at one time or another during the course of training, and that most everyone who sticks it out goes on to become a competent pilot.

The flat spots in the learning curve we're talking about are known as "learning plateaus." The phenomenon is formally taught to flight instructors because it occurs one or more times with every student they train. The student progresses rapidly for a while, then reaches a plateau with no apparent improvement. Once overcoming the plateau, it's back to rapid progress again.

There are a variety of approaches for getting past a learning plateau. Each of us learns differently, so sometimes it takes a few attempts to find one that works for a given student. If you feel that you and your instructor have "tried everything" with no results, take an extra lesson with someone else you respect, like your school's chief flight instructor. He or she may share another angle that illuminates it for you.

## Changing flight instructors midstream

Although your first instructor may well be the one you stay with, there is always the chance that his or her teaching style and your learning style may not match. In most cases, changing flight instructors is no big deal. You don't necessarily have to change flight schools or airports. Just talk to the chief flight instructor, tell him or her your concerns, and ask to be assigned to someone else. It happens all the time, and nobody the least bit mature should be upset about it. In fact, the flight school will appreciate your being honest and addressing it, rather than taking your business elsewhere.

If, however, you live near a small airport with only one instructor, your only option may be to travel to another airport to find a different one. Before making a change, be frank and try to guide your instructor to teach you in way that will match your own learning needs. Whatever you do, don't quit flying because of the instructor. There are plenty of good teachers out there; if necessary, make it your goal to find a better one.

## Keep the fun in your flying!

If, at some point during the training process, you do find yourself getting discouraged, it's time to take a break from the maneuvers and exercises and make

**C140 about to touch down at Georgetown, California**

a pleasure flight, to remind you of why you're pursuing that pilot certificate in the first place. For fun! For adventure! For relaxation!

Unless you already have an aviation background, your experience with flying may be limited to the intro flight, followed by a series of high-intensity lessons. Other than craning their necks for airplane traffic, few students get to savor the view prior to solo cross-country. That's why, even though it's not on the syllabus, there are times when a casual "pleasure flight" is the best thing you can do for yourself.

Ask your instructor to schedule an extra lesson to fly to an airport some distance away for lunch. Or, make the flight educational, and consider traveling to the nearest Flight Service Station (FSS) or radar approach control facility for a tour. You could also go to a "fly-in" (great for learning how to see and avoid other aircraft). Wherever you fly, make this trip long enough for some enjoyable flying, and allow time at the destination for you and your instructor to kick back, relax, and talk casually together.

Your pleasure flight objectives are twofold: to get some positive feedback on skills already learned, and to remind you of why it's worth the effort to become a pilot. A round-trip cross-country flight of even an hour gives you the chance to look out the window, stay on course, and maintain level flight.

It breaks the pattern of stressful lessons and gives you the opportunity to realize, "Hey, I may not have every maneuver perfectly nailed yet, but look at how far my flying has come. I just hopped in an airplane and flew it comfortably for a hundred miles, all while holding my heading and altitude, operating the radios, and having fun to boot. Imagine doing that a month ago!" In most cases you'll return from this pleasure trip encouraged, enthused, and rejuvenated.

# 7

# *About Airplanes and Flight*

## *T*he beauty of airplanes

When you watch an airplane lift off the ground and into the air, especially if it's a big airliner, it's easy to be awed. "How does that fly?" you might justifiably wonder. Unless you already know something about aerodynamics, it looks almost like magic. Luckily, you don't have to be a rocket scientist to know the answer. As a pilot, you will learn how airplane design makes it possible to fly. And the small airplane you will fly has a great deal in common with that big airliner.

The tapering body of every airplane is called the *fuselage*. It looks similar on most small aircraft and is made of light metals such as aluminum, or high-tech composites. Some airplanes have wings mounted above the fuselage; they are called *high-wing* airplanes. Others have wings below the fuselage and are called *low-wing* airplanes.

No matter where the wings are placed, they are all designed so that air passing over and under the wings creates lift. Even if the propeller stops, the airplane can glide to a landing, as long as the airflow over the wings is sufficient.

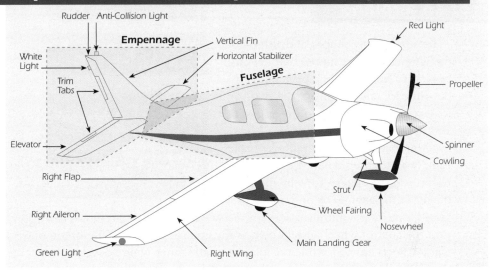

## Airplane 101: The basic parts of an airplane

Rudder
Anti-Collision Light
**Empennage**
Vertical Fin
Horizontal Stabilizer
Red Light
White Light
**Fuselage**
Trim Tabs
Propeller
Elevator
Spinner
Cowling
Right Flap
Strut
Right Aileron
Wheel Fairing
Nosewheel
Green Light
Right Wing
Main Landing Gear

Hinged to the wings are movable ailerons. When you, as pilot, turn the control wheel (or control yoke) left or right, these move up and down, in opposite directions, and bank the airplane left or right.

Also attached to the wings are movable flaps, controlled by an electrical switch or mechanical lever inside the airplane. As you've probably noticed in an airliner, flaps are usually extended during landing, because they add lift, create drag, and thereby help slow the airplane down so it uses less runway.

The tail of the airplane, also called the *empennage*, includes the fixed horizontal and vertical stabilizers. Among the moveable surfaces on the tail is the horizontal elevator, which the pilot controls by pushing the control wheel forward and pulling it back to direct the airplane's nose up and down. Another is the rudder, attached to the vertical stabilizer, which is controlled by pedals on the floor and moves the airplane's nose left and right. In light aircraft, rudder pedals have the additional function of steering the airplane while it's on the ground.

An airplane's landing gear includes the wheels and the struts that attach them to the airplane's fuselage. Most airplanes have a nosewheel near the front of the

## Flight controls of an airplane

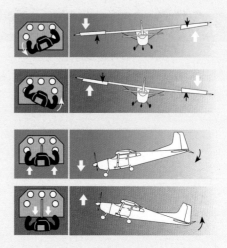

...are surprisingly simple, and although the systems may get more complex on larger airplanes, the basic principles are the same for anything from the two- or four-seater you learn in to the largest of airliners.

You may have wondered why planes bank (lean to one side) as they turn. The reason is that airplanes turn by directing the lift of their wings to one side. This is done by moving control surfaces on the wings known as ailerons. When you turn the control wheel (also known as the control yoke), the aileron on one wing deflects upward, while the aileron on the other wing goes down.

Climbing and descending is directed through use of movable control surfaces on the horizontal portion of the tail. Appropriately enough, they are called elevators and are activated by pushing the control wheel in and pulling it out.

The third basic control for flying an airplane is the rudder. Contrary to what you might expect, the rudder does not steer the plane but rather serves the purpose of properly aligning the plane in flight. The pilot controls the rudder's movement with rudder pedals on the floor of the airplane and also uses them to steer the airplane's nosewheel or tailwheel when on the ground.

So don't be alarmed when, on your first lesson, you discover that your instructor is taxiing the plane without moving the control wheel!

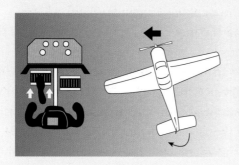

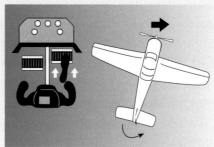

A "nosewheel" Cessna 182 and a "tailwheel" Citabria

airplane and two main wheels under the fuselage; these are called nosewheel, or tricycle-gear airplanes.

Although you will probably learn to fly in a nosewheel airplane, most of the traditional airplanes built before the 1950s were "taildraggers." That is, they had two main wheels under the fuselage and a smaller tailwheel (or, originally, a skid that dragged) at the back of the airplane. The older airplanes (many are still flying) and newer ones with that configuration are called tailwheel, or conventional-gear airplanes.

Part of your training will include learning what's under the cowling, or cover that encloses the engine that generates power to turn the propeller. Most aircraft engines are horizontally-opposed and air-cooled, much like the engine in the original Volkswagen beetle. If you're not an "under the hood" sort, here's your opportunity to gradually become one. It *is* important, if not essential, for you as a pilot to understand what makes the airplane tick. You won't have to master fixing it yourself, but the more you know about airplane engines and systems, the more skillful and confident you will be as a pilot.

Inside the cockpit, you will first notice all the switches, dials, and displays. The instrument panel may seem overwhelming at first, but soon you will learn to focus on the few indicators that are essential for basic flight. The others will become meaningful in time when you have accumulated some experience and are ready to use them. Eventually, you will balance your attention between the instruments inside the cockpit and the visual references outside the cockpit. Later in your training, you will learn how to fly relying solely on instruments as a safety measure, should you fly at night or in weather with low visibility.

Most trainer airplanes are equipped with only basic communication radios and navigational radios. Who, you may ask, does a pilot talk to, anyway? Well, many people, both on the ground and in the air. They include not only those in control towers but also radar controllers who direct traffic in the air and controllers of ground traffic at busy airports.

**Instrument panel in a Grumman Tiger**

## What are all those instruments about?

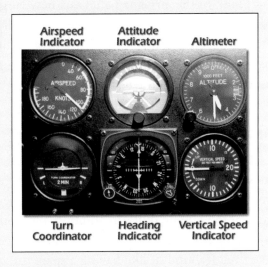

Airspeed Indicator  Attitude Indicator  Altimeter

Turn Coordinator  Heading Indicator  Vertical Speed Indicator

Despite the apparent complexity of an instrument panel at first glance, there are actually only six basic flight instruments used to pilot any kind of airplane, from the trainer you will learn in to an airline jet. Everything else is support equipment ranging from radios to controls for aircraft systems.

The "Basic Six" instruments in an airplane:

**Airspeed indicator** (or ASI) indicates the airplane's speed through the air, measured in knots or miles per hour.

**Altimeter** displays the airplane's altitude above sea level.

**Vertical speed indicator** (or VSI) indicates the rate at which the airplane is climbing or descending, in hundreds of feet per minute.

**Attitude indicator** displays the position of the airplane's nose and wings relative to the horizon.

**Heading indicator** (also called a directional gyro, or "DG") indicates the direction of the airplane's nose and is set by the pilot to align with the magnetic compass.

**Turn coordinator** guides the pilot in use of the rudder to properly balance turns.

A transponder mounted on the panel (usually a rectangular box with a four-digit display) sends out a radio signal with an assigned code to Air Traffic Control's (ATC) radar system that identifies you on their radar screen. Although you're only a blip, they know your altitude, how fast you're going and where you're headed. This is helpful when you want them to assist you in staying on course or alert you to the position of other airplanes in your area.

Think of the airplane panel as a new language you are about to learn. Take it one instrument, or word, at a time. Eventually, you learn a phrase, then a sentence and, ultimately, a valuable new means of communication. The airplane's instruments and gauges provide information that will help you understand the fascinating language of aviation.

## Are small airplanes really safe?

Once you start flying, don't be surprised if many people ask you that question. Be assured, today's aircraft are extremely reliable, and mechanical failures are rare. The airplanes that you will fly are designed to stay airborne and glide to earth, if the engine quits. In addition, most airplanes have redundant systems, both in engine and instrument operation. That is, if one fails, there's another one to take over. It's kind of like having a spare tire *and* a cell phone.

It's worth mentioning, however, that one form of mechanical failure does result in a considerable number of forced landings and accidents—engine failure from "fuel mismanagement." In short, the pilot ran out of gas. Whose fault was that? Good judgment and planning are the keys to avoiding that mistake.

Unlike cars, airplanes must be repaired by mechanics specifically certified by the FAA. While private pilots can do certain preventive maintenance, such as changing oil and replacing spark plugs, every airplane that flies is required to have regular inspections by a federally licensed mechanic. Thanks to these high standards of maintenance and care, airplane accidents due to mechanical failure seldom occur.

## Learning about flight

As a child, you may have held a toy airplane and pretended it could fly. You moved it up and down, left and right, on its side, upside down. You made the sounds of a motor revving up, taking off, getting louder and softer.

Unlike other vehicles, airplanes operate in a three-dimensional medium. The experience is like no other. Visualizing the airplane moving through the air, and the air as a force affecting the airplane, is part of learning to fly.

Airflow over and under the airplane's wings creates lift. Of course, the wings

## Are the airplanes I'll fly reliable?

Simple as light airplanes might appear, they are equipped with some pretty sophisticated safety systems. Let's consider the engine for one example. Although most light airplanes use piston engines related to those found in cars, there are some major additional safety features.

For example, you probably know that your car has a spark plug in each cylinder to ignite fuel and drive the engine. That device produces sparks using electricity generated through the car's electrical system. Since most of us don't savor the idea of an engine failure while flying, aircraft engines are equipped with two spark plugs in every cylinder, each driven by entirely separate ignition systems. Even in the unlikely event of losing one ignition system, the engine continues to run on the other one. (Try that in a car!) What's more, the spark plugs in airplanes are powered by magnetos rather than the battery electrical system. So, unlike cars, if an airplane's battery fails, the engine does not quit.

Given safety features like these, modern airplane engines are very reliable. In fact the most common reason they quit is not so different from today's reliable cars—

**Six-cylinder engine in a Piper Dakota**

"fuel starvation." That's right, the most common reason for airplane engines to fail is because pilots run them out of gas. And that's indeed as dumb as it sounds.

What happens if the engine does quit, for whatever reason? Simple, just glide down and land. You'll learn the proper techniques for this along with other safety procedures during flight training.

of an airplane, no matter what the shape, are designed to keep the airplane airborne. An airplane is also designed to be maneuverable and controllable, so when you move the control wheel and rudder pedals, it responds as you expect it to. The faster the airplane flies, the quicker and more dramatically it responds to your control input, like the quicker response of a car on the freeway versus driving slowly on a residential street.

As you roll down the runway, you'll ease the airplane into the air when your airspeed is sufficient for takeoff. For pilots, lifting off the ground is one of the most thrilling sensations in the world. When you have reached your desired altitude, you lower the nose and "level off" to cruise. Your turns to the left or right will require both your hands and your feet to control the ailerons and rudder. As with skiing, or anything else that requires coordination, you'll develop the perfect balance with practice.

Your flight training will begin with simple maneuvers, like climbs, descents and shallow turns. Then you'll learn steeper turns, S-turns across a road or other straight reference line along the ground, slow flight, and stalls. You will practice many takeoffs and landings, including the skills for short and soft runways, for crosswinds on windy days, and for calm days. You will even learn to like, or at least be comfortable with, turbulence. Sitting at the controls on a bumpy day is like being the driver of a car or motorcycle on a twisting road—you can see the curves and bumps coming, so it's no big deal. Quickly, you'll learn to appreciate the joy of being the pilot, steering through the air from the front seat.

## The risks of being a pilot

If you haven't asked yourself the question, someone else surely will: "Aren't you afraid to be up there?" Flying is not without risk; the mere fact of being elevated from the ground makes this activity relatively unforgiving of mistakes. The good news, however, is that through use of good judgment pilots can very effectively manage that risk.

What's the one thing about driving that scares you most? It may take a moment's thought, but almost everyone answers this question in the same way: "What frightens me most about driving is that somebody going the other way will cross the centerline just as I come over a hill," or "that some jerk will pull out in front of me when I least suspect it." Since mid-air collisions are rare, flying largely eliminates the greatest fear of drivers—fear of "the other guy." In short, with flying you are almost totally in control of your own destiny.

With that in mind, it's worth discussing the most common causes of aircraft accidents. One is doing stunts near the ground; for example, ill-advised feats like buzzing a friend's house, or flying up blind canyons in mountainous terrain.

It's no wonder that these are life-shortening activities because flying at low altitude largely defines risk in airplanes. When you think about it, there's little danger of hitting anything at altitude. Down low, however, there's no shortage of things to run into. Not only are there obvious hazards to avoid, like hills and buildings, but also many obstacles barely visible from the air, if at all. Wires, towers, poles, and fences are among the worst offenders.

Another statistically serious threat to aviators is flying into *known bad weather*. Weather hazards include such threats to light plane safety as fog, thunderstorms, and accumulation of ice on the airplane. The most common weather hazard threatening pilots who have not yet earned their instrument ratings is flight into

reduced visibility areas such as clouds, haze, and precipitation. This is pretty alarming stuff. Notice, however, that we said "known bad weather." Let us emphasize the word, *known*. In the vast majority of weather-related accidents the pilot received plenty of warning ahead of time as to the existence of hazardous weather, but *decided to proceed anyway*.

Why in the world would people take such risks, with so much at stake? That's an important question to ask yourself as you start the road to becoming a pilot. Unfortunately, even intelligent and reasonable people sometimes allow the pressures of business appointments, family obligations, and "get-home-itis" to override legitimate safety concerns. There's a lesson in that for all of us. Only those who have the self-confidence and willingness to occasionally make tough decisions to abort their missions should become pilots.

In other words, flying is a safe as you decide to make it. As the pilot, you are in command of a high percentage of the variables that affect the safety of flight. You will decide how much fuel to take, what type of weather to fly in, how the aircraft will be maintained, and where to fly. With good training, prudent judgment, and excellent equipment, you can operate at a very high level of safety. Pilots who properly plan their trips, ensure that there's enough fuel in the plane to get to their destinations, refrain from low-level stunts, and avoid *known* bad weather, can anticipate many years of safe and enjoyable flying.

Most people interested in learning to fly are the type who are confident of their own skills; once they understand that they will largely control their own safety, they usually feel pretty good about it.

Finally, the more you learn, the more at ease you'll be in an airplane. The mystery will disappear, and your appreciation for the "magic" will grow. Taking an airplane into the sky and landing it safely on the ground is an accomplishment, and it doesn't come without the real-time experience of flying.

## The big picture

Once you're comfortable being in the air, the bigger picture of what flying offers will emerge. For instance, there are over 5,000 public airports for you to choose from. Wow!

How do you find them? Well, aeronautical charts, just like road maps and

**Wind indicator and ramp at Auburn, California**

topographical maps, cover every inch of the country with details about terrain, lakes and rivers, cities and small towns, and, of course, airports. Published flight guides provide even more information about the airports, such as their facilities and services.

Learning radio communication skills is a necessary part of your flight training. If you learn to fly at a busy airport, you'll quickly become accustomed to talking and listening carefully whenever you're in the air. If you take lessons at a small airport, your communication may be limited to talking with the few other pilots using the airport.

When you first hear radio communications between Air Traffic Control and a pilot, it may sound like gobbledygook. A whirl of numbers and letters flies back and forth interspersed with words and abbreviations that don't seem to make sense. For example, a pilot may say, "Oakland Center, three-niner-six-seven-

## The Alpha-Bravo-Charlies of flying:

"Toledo Tower, this is Cessna five-nine-three-bee-tee. Over."

"Say again. Was that Cessna nine-five-three-pee-dee?"

"Negative. This is five-nine-three-bee-tee."

That's how radio conversation between a pilot and a controller would sound without a phonetic alphabet. Aviators use numbers and letters in most radio communications with control towers, radar operators, weather briefers, and each other. It has long been recognized that some letters sound confusingly similar to each other when transmitted by radio (the letters b, c, d, e, g, p, t and z, for example). To address this problem, the letters are given names, such as "bravo" for B and "tango" for "T." The number nine is pronounced "niner," and numbers over nine are read as individual digits, such as "three-zero" for 30 and "one-two-two-point-eight" for 122.8.

Now, that same radio conversation begins much more smoothly like this:

"Toledo Tower, this is Cessna five-niner-three-bravo-tango. Over."

"Go ahead, three-bravo-tango." (Only the last three characters need be used after the initial call-up is made and understood.)

| Phonetic Alphabet | |
|---|---|
| A | Alfa (ALFAH) |
| B | Bravo (BRAHVOH) |
| C | Charlie (CHAR-LEE or SHAR-LEE) |
| D | Delta (DELL-TA) |
| E | Echo (ECK-OH) |
| F | Foxtrot (FOKS-TROT) |
| G | Golf (GOLF) |
| H | Hotel (HOH-TEL) |
| I | India (IN-DEE-AH) |
| J | Juliet (JOO-LEE-ETT) |
| K | Kilo (KEY-LOH) |
| L | Lima (LEE-MAH) |
| M | Mike (MIKE) |
| N | November (NO-VEM-BER) |
| O | Oscar (OSS-CAH) |
| P | Papa (PAH-PAH) |
| Q | Quebec (KEH-BECK) |
| R | Romeo (ROW-ME-OH) |
| S | Sierra (SEE-AIR-AH) |
| T | Tango (TANG-GO) |
| U | Uniform (YOU-NEE-FORM) |
| V | Victor (VIK-TAH) |
| W | Whiskey (WISS-KEY) |
| X | Xray (ECKS-RAY) |
| Y | Yankee (YANG-KEY) |
| Z | Zulu (ZOO-LOO) |
| 1 | One (WUN) |
| 2 | Two (TOO) |
| 3 | Three (TREE) |
| 4 | Four (FOW-ER) |
| 5 | Five (FIFE) |
| 6 | Six (SIX) |
| 7 | Seven (SEVEN) |
| 8 | Eight (AIT) |
| 9 | Niner (NIN-ER) |
| 0 | Zero (ZEE-RO) |

If you really want to impress your flight instructor, along with your other new pilot friends, memorize the phonetic alphabet ahead of time. Not only will it come in handy on the radio, but it's better than pig Latin for mystifying non-pilots at social gatherings.

**Exploring the bush country in New Zealand's Southern Alps**

victor, two-zero miles northeast of Auburn Airport, VFR Santa Rosa, request flight following." Oakland Center (ATC) may reply, "three-niner-six-seven-victor, squawk three-three-six-eight. Sacramento altimeter two-niner-niner-seven. Radar contact two-zero miles northeast of Auburn." Whew!

You're probably thinking, "I'll *never* learn how to do that!" But, you will, and, in fact, it's great fun. You will learn that there's a predictable order to the information and that everyone uses the same aviation language, such as the phonetic alphabet.

Preparing you to make good decisions on your own is your flight instructor's goal from the very first lesson. For example, when you call for a weather briefing prior to a cross-country flight, not only will you receive current weather information, you will also get the forecast for your route of flight and for your destination. Weather decisions, or "go/no-go" decisions, are the most challenging for any pilot, especially a new one.

Your weather knowledge will also enhance your navigational skills. Planning a cross-country flight includes plotting the route to your destination as well as calculating your arrival time, based on current and forecast weather. Most pilots enjoy the process of analyzing charts and flight guides. It's not unlike drawing lines on a road map or nautical chart in preparation for a trip that you're eager to take.

If you continue beyond your Private Pilot certificate to take advanced flight training for your instrument rating, then your weather decisions will expand in scope. Instrument-rated pilots can legally fly in weather without being able to see the ground, that is, in the clouds. They follow Instrument Flight Rules (IFR) and have learned how to use their instruments to give them all the information they need to fly safely. Until then, you will be a VFR pilot, following Visual Flight Rules, which essentially means you must be able to see the ground to fly.

For a pilot, preparation is everything. If you've done your homework, planned your route, studied the airport information, reviewed your airplane's manual, and received a weather briefing, you are ready to fly. You will learn something new almost every time you fly, but, being well informed ahead of time, you'll be far better prepared to handle any unexpected situations along the way. The more you fly, the more you'll learn to enjoy it, too. Like anything worthwhile; it takes time and effort to be a good pilot, and there's no substitute for experience.

# 8

# *What You Can Do Once You're a Pilot*

*A*fter months of hard work, the day the examiner hands you your Private Pilot certificate you will be *soaring*, with or without an airplane! That initial euphoria will be followed by overwhelming joy when you realize that you are now *free to fly* whenever, wherever, and with whomever you choose. Yet, that freedom carries with it a responsibility to try to improve every time you takeoff and land. What you have really earned is a "license to learn."

## When does my Private Pilot certificate expire?

Private Pilot certificates never expire. If you don't fly for a few months, or even a year, after earning your license, all you will need to do is go up with an instructor to get familiar again with the airplane. You will want to refresh your memory on airport operations and airspace, of course. In order to comply with FAA regulations, you must make three takeoffs and landings every 90 days before carrying passengers. If that 90-day period passes without three takeoffs and landings, you will need to make them solo, or with an instructor, before you can take passengers.

Federal regulations also require that all pilots have a "flight review" every two years, which includes a minimum of one hour of flight training and one hour of ground training with an instructor who will endorse your logbook. So, if it's been two years or more since you earned your license, you will need a flight review, which may require some additional flight training with an instructor to renew your flying skills. (A new certificate or rating can also satisfy the flight review requirement.)

You will always need to carry your pilot certificate and a current (i.e., unexpired) medical certificate to legally pilot an airplane.

## After earning my certificate, how often must I fly to maintain my skills?

"Is it like driving a car or riding a bicycle in that once I learn it I won't forget the basics like takeoffs and landings?" you might ask.

Flying is indeed a skill that stays with you like learning to ride a bike. But pilots do get rusty if they don't fly regularly, especially if they don't have much experience to begin with. After earning your Private Pilot certificate, you should try to fly at least briefly every week or two, especially until you get some experience under your belt.

The good news is that, once you earn your license, the cost of flying regularly is probably less than you think. You can do a few turns around the pattern in as little as a half hour or 45 minutes, and get useful practice out of it.

More importantly, as a private pilot you can often share expenses with your passengers. (Federal regulations spell out the details.) So, stay sharp by doing some

If you have in mind to become a professional pilot, whether as an instructor, corporate pilot, or airline pilot, you'll need advanced instruction to acquire more certificates and ratings, as well as additional flight time.

Along with qualifying you for personal flying, becoming a private pilot is also the first step toward flying professionally, should you ever decide to pursue it. The Private Pilot certificate is the cornerstone of every civilian piloting career from flight instructor to airline captain and everything in between. So get started with your Private Pilot training, knowing that the door will always be open for you to continue after completing it. The normal course of advancement toward a professional pilot career goes more or less like this:

1. Private Pilot certificate
2. Instrument rating
3. Commercial Pilot certificate
4. Multiengine rating
5. Flight Instructor certificate (multiple ratings may be added)
6. Airline Transport Pilot certificate
7. Specific "type ratings" for flying large and jet-powered aircraft

Even pilots not seeking to fly professionally often choose to continue their training to increase skill and proficiency. (The instrument rating in particular is valuable for almost every pilot.) Note that "certificates" are basic pilot licenses while "ratings" are qualifications added to those licenses (like the adding of motorcycle operating privileges to an automobile driver's license).

Advanced ratings and certificates can be earned one-by-one through most flight schools, or may be pursued in a more comprehensive manner through integrated training programs offered at private and university flight academies.

affordable flying for the fun of it. That's why you're getting your license, right? Pick some exciting places you want to go, invite a friend or two to go along, and split the cost.

If you must miss a few weeks or a month without flying, however, don't worry; all of your skills won't evaporate. Just get back into that airplane as soon as you reasonably can, and, if in doubt about your proficiency, go up for a session

**Airport sunset over West Yellowstone, Montana**

with your instructor to brush up. Good pilots do that sort of thing all the time. Adding ratings and certificates is another terrific way to stay sharp. Each advanced rating or certificate reinforces the old one.

## What if I'm not 100 percent confident after earning my pilot certificate?

Although competent on the day they pass their tests, many new pilots are a bit nervous for a while after earning their certificates. For that reason, it's often helpful and fun for new aviators to team up with other pilots of similar experience for planning and flying together. That also saves money while both are

getting more comfortable with the whole business. While one of you is busy with the flying, the other can handle the radio. And, when tough decisions come up, two heads are available to discuss things, like weather challenges. It's important to remember, however, that *only one* person can legally, or practically, be pilot-in-command (PIC) on any given flight. That pilot takes full responsibility for the safe outcome of the trip and who it is should be determined *before* you both get in the airplane. In flight is *not* the time to decide who's in charge.

Many newly-minted pilots think that, once they're licensed, they are expected to know "everything" and don't need to fly with an instructor. This couldn't be further from the truth. Even airline captains must by law fly with an instructor every six months. Your instructor knows that you're relatively new at being a pilot; he or she will be delighted if you call for a flight together now and then.

Consider additional crosswind landing, night, or instrument training. Even one lesson on any of those will enhance your skills and increase your confidence a great deal.

Take advantage of your instructor to get "checked out" in additional aircraft models, that is, to be familiarized with airplanes different from the one you're accustomed to flying. The checkout will be easy but, at the same time, a great review of the basics. Besides, you may even find yourself more comfortable in another model, and you'll then have additional planes to choose from when you fly.

Finally, it helps to understand that most pilots' confidence erodes long before their competence does. In other words, the longer you go without flying, the less confident you feel about going back to it. But, the actual flying ability of those same pilots stays good for quite a long time; at worst, a brush-up and they're as sharp as ever! The best way to become more self-assured as a pilot is simply to do more flying.

So, after becoming a pilot, head out to the airport often for a "fix" with an aviator friend or your instructor. And even with all this talk about training, make sure that all of those trips are about fun!

## How can I get my family and friends excited about flying?

One of the great pleasures of flying, for most pilots, is sharing the joy with others. It is absolutely imperative that, as part of your captain's duties, you make flying a wonderful experience for your passengers. In many respects, you must give first-time passengers "demo flights," in the sense of the introductory lesson you took yourself several chapters ago.

Giving their first airplane ride is a day that pilots look forward to throughout their training, yet often their lucky new passengers have been dreading it. Likely as not, those passengers haven't flown much, if ever, in a light plane. Since their new pilot once dinged the family car, or can't fix a broken sink, or sometimes forgets to turn off the porch light before going to bed, family members sometimes feel that their new aviator can't possibly have what it takes to be a pilot.

The appropriate skills to demonstrate when giving a first flight are smoothness, professionalism, great takeoffs and landings, and, perhaps, cross-

country ability. Prior to cranking up the engine, pilots of first-time passengers should always spend a few moments explaining what's going to happen through the taxi and takeoff experience.

One mark of a professional pilot everyone can relate to is the preflight briefing. After all, that's what happens every time a passenger gets on an airliner, isn't it? So, along with the regulatory obligations of a pilot to brief passengers before flying, there's also an opportunity to share additional information (such as the purpose of the flashing transponder reply light and beeping stall warning horn), which both demonstrates the pilot's confidence and helps to put passengers at ease.

Never give someone a first ride on a day when a rough ride is likely, nor when the weather looks threatening. However, if despite your best efforts, it turns out that you might encounter some turbulence, point it out to your passengers ahead of time.

"See those hills up there, Barb? Since there's wind flowing over them from the west, we may experience a few bumps till we get to the other side." If turbulence does exist over those hills, the passengers know what to expect, so the experience will be less traumatic. And if the air is smooth, well, they'll be impressed by their knowledgeable pilot all the same.

Compare for a moment piloting airplanes to riding motorcycles. Driving a motorcycle is a blast, but riding on the back is a drag, because the passenger is totally out of control. Your passengers will have the same reaction to a wild first airplane flight, as does the back-seat rider on a scary motorcycle ride.

As a new private pilot you have just spent many hours mastering flight maneuvers in airplanes, and you should be justifiably proud of doing it. But those are *not* the skills to demonstrate on the first flight with the family. It may sound obvious, but a surprising number of new pilots try to impress passengers with their newly-acquired flying skills by performing stalls and steep turns. This can be an extremely serious mistake, because once family members have become frightened of flying, they probably won't do it again.

Ideally, on your first flight, you'll choose a destination your passenger would love to visit. Take your girlfriend to lunch. Meet your husband's folks for breakfast. In short, fly somewhere in an hour that would be too far to drive. Make a trip to a place that's a special experience made possible by flying.

Later on after a few flights together, you might involve your passengers in planning the flight, locating airport information in the flight guide, and navigating using the charts to identify landmarks. Having a useful role can make their flying experience more enjoyable.

Those friends or family members who fly with you often may want to invest in a "Flying Companion" seminar, video or book. The seminars can be as short as four hours and as long as a weekend. Look around to see if there's one available in your area.

## Can I afford to continue flying?

Interestingly enough, many people who think they can't afford flying are not concerned about the initial cost of the lessons. That may sound strange, but it comes back to another of those misconceptions about being a pilot. Many people

**Ski plane above Mt. Cook, New Zealand**

gather through the grapevine that pilots must continually practice and retrain to maintain their skills. This is indeed true and, in fact, is the mark of a good pilot. But, prospective pilots often think that the cost and time investments required to "stay current" are orders of magnitude greater than they actually are.

What's more, people often think flying will be prohibitively expensive even when the lessons are over. We simply cannot address the cost of flying without giving some examples of what a great deal flying is *after* you've earned your certificate!

Let's use as an example a basic four-seat single-engine airplane renting for $90 per hour. Say you and your spouse want to visit a getaway that's 280 road miles away, and you're taking along another couple.

These aircraft typically cruise at around 140 miles per hour, so the four of you can be at your destination in only two hours, versus four to five hours each way driving, depending on road conditions. Since you pay plane rental only for the time while the engine is running, and the hourly rate includes fuel, the total round-trip cost per person to fly there works out to about $90.

Now think about this. Not only will everyone still be fresh when getting to your destination, but you won't have to pay for a hotel room and take an extra day off as when you drive there. In addition, you may find a way to incorporate flying in your job, especially if you travel and need to be somewhere that usually requires driving or taking a commercial flight.

There are also volunteer opportunities for your flying skills, including worthy organizations like Angel Flight. Consider joining the local squadron of Civil Air Patrol. As a mission pilot you'll have opportunities to fly for free, and it's for a good cause. Other ways to make flying pay are available: flying parachute jumpers, ferrying airplanes, towing gliders, flight instructing, and taking aerial photographs. These jobs may require that you add ratings beyond your Private Pilot certificate but that could be another enjoyable process that will greatly enhance your flying skills. Many flight schools welcome part-time instructors, a rewarding profession, and the flying is "free." Some part-timers throw their instructing income into a pot for personal flying. That way all their flying pays for itself.

Where there's a will, there's a way. If it's a priority, you'll find ways to keep flying. And, if it remains important in your life, you'll never regret the time or money you've invested in flying.

## Must I take a test for every different kind of airplane I fly?

Most people learn to fly in single-engine airplanes. But not all single-engine airplanes are equal, and, when you're ready to move up, the government requires that you get special training to fly some of them. In most cases, this will simply require flying with an instructor who will "endorse" your logbook.

For example, if you want to fly airplanes with 200 hp or more, you will need a high-performance airplane endorsement from an authorized instructor. To earn that, you must fly with an instructor in a high-performance airplane until he or

**Aeronca Chief on floats, Elliot Lake, Ontario**

she determines that you are proficient to pilot an airplane with the additional power. Depending on the model, it may take only an hour or two for you to be "signed off" with your one-time endorsement to legally fly high-performance airplanes. Many high-performance airplanes are not much different to fly than the trainer airplane you will learn in.

Flying complex airplanes, which have retractable landing gear, flaps, and a controllable propeller, also requires ground and flight training from an instructor. Again, you will receive a one-time "complex airplane" endorsement when the instructor determines that you are proficient to act as PIC.

An endorsement is also required to fly tailwheel airplanes. An instructor will teach you how to make both "three-point" and "wheel" landings, along with crosswind takeoffs and landings in a tailwheel airplane before endorsing your logbook. Then, just as with your Private Pilot certificate, you'll never have to take the test again. It doesn't mean, of course, that you won't need a refresher someday, but it won't require another endorsement.

## Where should I go and what should I do as a new pilot?

Are you kidding? There's a whole world out there to explore! For many of us, what makes a given flight really fun is having a mission. Pilots, and their passengers, might hem and haw about hopping into the plane to fly around locally just for fun. But when it comes to a real mission, like picking up the kids from summer camp, now *that's* exciting!

Many flight schools and flying clubs organize

group flights using multiple airplanes. Often it's set up in the form of a once-per-month outings, where pilots and their families travel somewhere by plane for activities ranging from fly-in breakfasts to ski weekends. You'll find many ideas for interesting fly-in destinations in pilot magazines such as *Pilot Getaways*.

Another great way to keep both the fun and learning in your flying is to ask more experienced pilots to invite you along on flights that will expose you to new situations and more advanced aircraft. For example, if a pilot needs to do some hood work (practice instrument flying), offer to go along as safety pilot (watching for other airplanes). It's a great way to begin learning about instrument flight, plus you get to log the flight time as a "required crew member."

For that matter, whenever you can, ask to go along on a "real" (as opposed to simulated) flight through the clouds. Few non-instrument rated pilots have ever experienced flight "in the soup." Most don't even know what instrument flying is about and can't imagine why they might want to take instrument lessons one day. But, your first experience flying through clouds will grip your interest right up to

**Twin-engine Piper Apache over the Sierra Nevada foothills**

**A pilot's view of the Grand Prismatic Pool, Yellowstone National Park**

the grand finale of bursting from the overcast over the runway at your destination. Instrument flying is such a kick that you may instantly take to it, though you might never consider it without being invited along.

Since night training requirements for the Private Pilot certificate are limited, new pilots tend to be apprehensive about flying at night when they complete their checkrides. So, corral your instructor whenever possible for night proficiency and night cross-country flights.

Continue to call on your instructor for advice after earning your pilot certificate. Got a trip coming up, and you'd like another opinion on a tough weather decision? Phone your trusty flight instructor! Print out a copy of the weather and go over it together.

## Will I be ready to fly long trips when I become a pilot?

When you complete your training and earn your Private Pilot certificate, you should have all the basic skills required for a flight around the country. Exciting, eh?

To prepare yourself for that big trip, it's a good idea to make some shorter cross-country trips first, in order to gain experience and confidence. Also, long trips across the country require a good understanding of weather and the ability to interpret it, which includes some background in the localized conditions

found in different parts of the country, such as fog near areas of water and the effects of wind and density altitude in mountainous areas.

So, in preparation for that first big adventure flight, read all you can about flying in various conditions and consult with other pilots who have flown in those areas before. Each airport landing is an opportunity to meet other pilots who can share local knowledge and tips about flying in their area, often to your next destination. With a bit of experience under your belt, and your homework out of the way, that trip across the country will be exhilarating and enjoyable.

Finally, perhaps the most important thing on long trips is not to impose any tight timetable on yourself. The biggest safety consideration on most cross-country flights is weather. On each day of the journey, you must put yourself in the mode of "If we don't like the weather today, we'll wait until it improves before continuing," even if that means staying where you are for another day or two, or longer. That attitude adds tremendously to the safety of a long cross-country trip because, if you don't go rushing into adverse weather, your problems should be minimal. Some of your most memorable flying adventures will include interesting experiences at unplanned stops. Relax and enjoy it!

## Should I buy an airplane?

Many aviators happily rent airplanes for a lifetime of enjoyable flying. But, of course, for a pilot, owning an airplane rates right at the top of the list.

It's true that airplanes can be costly to own and keep. But, like anything, it's relative. You can find a vintage, two-place airplane for half the price of a new SUV, or invest half-a-million or more in the latest high-tech sleek machine. And, then, there's everything in-between. Of course, you'll first want to investigate the expense of owning an airplane including maintenance, repairs, hangar fees, fuel and oil, and insurance. The good news is that many airplanes appreciate over time. For example, many 20-year-old airplanes are worth double what they originally cost, hundreds or thousands of enjoyable flying hours later.

Common wisdom says that if you plan to fly between 100 and 150 hours a year and would rent an airplane to do that, then you could justify owning one. If you can deduct any of the airplane expenses for business, and are flying frequently, then you have another reason to own one. Keep in mind that, although you can estimate the annual expense of owning and operating an airplane, you can't always predict when it will need a major repair, so cash flow issues should figure in your planning.

Sharing ownership of an airplane is another good option for pilots, usually through partnerships or flying clubs. AOPA has a very useful member website

## What does it cost to operate your own airplane?

By now you're probably wondering about the cost of owning and operating your own airplane. As with cars, boats, houses, or other major capital investments, the most important aspect when investing in an airplane is to ensure that the model you select fits your budget. With airplanes, that includes not only the purchase price but also operating costs.

The following is a useful worksheet for calculating the cost of owning your own dream airplane. Notice that, with airplanes, the fixed costs are a major part of ownership; therefore, the more you fly a plane, the less each hour of flight costs.

### Checklist for calculating the annual cost of aircraft ownership and operation.

**Annual Costs**

Hangar or tiedown fees          $ _____

Insurance                       $ _____

Annual inspection               $ _____
(required by federal regulations)

**Direct Hourly Costs**

Fuel and Oil                    $ _____

Mechanical and avionics allowance★    $ _____

★Obviously, maintenance costs are not 100 percent predictable, so many aircraft owners set aside funds to cover these costs when needed.

Engine reserve★★                $ _____

★★Unlike cars that are usually disposed of when the engine fails, airplanes last a very long time. Therefore, aircraft owners overhaul or replace their engines, after a 1500- to 2400-hour life. If you buy a used airplane, the TSMOH (time since major overhaul) on the engine should be considered, as that will give you an idea of how close you might be to facing a significant expense.

that includes questions and answers you'll need to know before agreeing to co-ownership.

Suggest to ardent airplane owners that airplanes aren't affordable, and they'll shake their heads and mumble something like "You're crazy" and that giving it up is like selling a child. *Not* an option.

The beauty of owning your own airplane is that it provides flexibility in your flight planning, it's always there when you want it, you know how it flies, and that's it's been well cared for and maintained. Instantly, you become a member of a special club of airplane owners who will embrace you for sharing their passion.

## *You can fly!*

Believing that *you can fly*, working hard and dedicating yourself to the goal ahead are the first steps to earning the special badge of being a pilot. Buying an airplane gives you the *ultimate* freedom to "slip the surly bonds of earth" and discover a whole new world of travel and adventure that has no bounds. One thing is certain, whether you rent planes or buy your own—your life will have changed.

Enough reading, get out and start flying!

## Answers to Your Aviation Questions

### 1. How fast are we going?

If you've ever asked a pilot that question when riding in an airplane, you probably got a confusing answer. Airplanes are more like boats in the way they move than like cars. When a car drives at 50 mph, that's its speed no matter how you might define it. If a boat or plane travels at a fixed speed through water or air, however, there's another factor involved since neither is connected directly to the ground. That is, how fast is the water or air itself moving?

When a 40-mph boat travels upstream against a 10-mph current, its actual speed past the nearby shore is only 30 mph. If, however, the boater gets frustrated and turns around, that same 40-mph boat will now pass the shore at 50 mph, traveling downstream. The difference, of course, is in the speed of the water.

The same applies in airplanes, and to differentiate

between speed through the air and speed over the ground, different terms are required: airspeed and groundspeed. As you might expect, "true airspeed" and "groundspeed" are equal when there's no wind. Otherwise they're different. Most likely when you asked the pilot "How fast are we going?" what you really wanted to know was "What's our groundspeed?" meaning speed over the ground.

The airplane's "airspeed indicator" (corresponding to a car's speedometer) will only tell you the speed of the airplane through the air. "Groundspeed" must be read from an electronic device like a GPS, or else calculated using one of several simple methods. Now you know why the pilot hesitated before answering that question, though as an aviator you'll soon master those details yourself.

## 2. How high are we?

Along with "How fast are we going?" pilots and passengers are always interested in knowing "How high are we?" Altimeters work on the principle that atmospheric air gets thinner as one increases altitude from sea level. By measuring air density at any given moment, an altimeter determines how high you are. The figure at left shows an airplane altimeter.

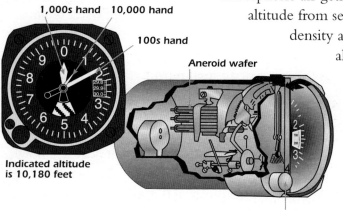

1,000s hand   10,000 hand

100s hand

Aneroid wafer

Indicated altitude is 10,180 feet

Altimeter setting knob

So now you know how high you are, but how high above what? At first glance, it might seem logical that an airplane's altimeter would display height above the ground. But that doesn't work well for flying, it turns out, because the ground at any given location is likely at a different elevation than that somewhere else. Since the most important function of an altimeter is to keep planes from running into the ground or each other, it's important that all their altimeters use the same reference point.

For that reason aircraft altimeters display height above sea level, rather than height above ground. Strange as it may sound upon first hearing it, an airplane sitting on the ground at Chicago displays an altitude of around 600 feet, while one on the ground at the Santa Fe, New Mexico, airport displays 6,200 feet. It all makes sense, however, once they take flight.

Regardless of where any two airplanes might have departed from, their altimeters are on the same

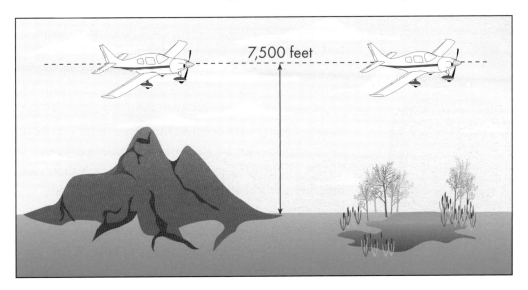

7,500 feet

reference with each other and with the ground obstructions marked on the map in height above sea level.

## 3. What are these "knots" I keep hearing about?

There are two kinds of miles used in aviation. "Statute miles" are land-based miles of the variety U.S. drivers use in cars. "Nautical miles" originated in boat navigation and are slightly larger than statute miles. (One nautical mile is 6,076 feet; one statute mile is 5,280 feet.)

When pilots talk speed, the term "miles per hour" translates to "statute miles per hour." Nautical miles per hour are referred to instead as "knots." (This term dates back to the days when sailing ships measured velocity by timing the passage of knots on a rope thrown overboard.)

You'll hear all these terms in use out at the airport. When calculating speed and distance, modern aviators most often measure their progress in knots and nautical miles. Those are the units marked on today's airspeed indicators, and in which winds are reported.

Some pilots, however, still do their planning using statute miles. That's because the airspeed indicators on older airplanes are often marked in miles per hour. "Miles per hour" also remains popular in aircraft sales brochures and among speed-driven aviators who build their own airplanes. Do the math and you'll see why. One knot (one nautical mile per hour) equals approximately 1.15 statute miles per hour. What makes better boasting—140 knots or 160 miles per hour?

## 4. How do pilots know where they are?

Today's pilots use a combination of three different methods to determine position and progress toward a destination.

The most obvious way of navigating is simply looking out the window and noting what's on the ground. **Pilotage**, or flying by reference to visual landmarks, is the earliest form of aerial navigation and still relevant today. By looking out the window and identifying roads, towns, lakes and rivers, mountain peaks, even prominent buildings along your route, you confirm that you are "on course" to your destination. Many trips can be completed simply by following a road, river, or railroad track to your destination. Aeronautical charts are specifically designed to make such navigation easy.

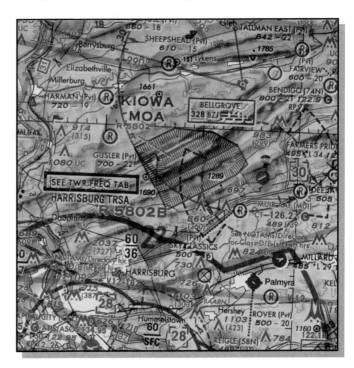

**Dead reckoning** involves making simple calculations to predict the plane's speed and adjust the direction of flight based on prevailing winds. This method was developed for flight when few landmarks are visible. Dead reckoning can be surprisingly accurate and is, for example, how Charles Lindbergh remained on course while crossing the Atlantic Ocean in 1927. After 24 hours over water, he crossed the coast of Ireland within a few miles of his intended landfall. The method is so effective that pilots still learn it today.

**Electronic navigation** involves using electronic devices to locate your plane's position and guide it to its destination. During your lessons you will learn about a variety of navigational devices. GPS (global positioning system), in particular, has made navigating airplanes so simple that few pilots get lost anymore, nor will you when you learn to fly. Even the smallest handheld GPS displays your airplane's position on a moving map, along with a line defining the plane's course to its destination.

## 5. What's with those numbers painted on the side of the plane?

Every airplane has a combination of numbers and letters painted on its side that identifies it, like a license plate on a car. The first letter or two refer to the aircraft's country of registration. ("N" designates U.S.-registered aircraft.)

This registration number also serves as the airplane's "call sign," or name for purposes of radio communication. Using the aviation phonetic alphabet, the pilot of "N3967V" would identify the airplane she's flying as "November-three-niner-six-seven-victor."

## 6. Which way is North?

It may sound like a simple enough question, but, in actuality, pilots learn to navigate based on two different kinds of north. Look at a world globe, and you can easily pick out the North Pole. That's what's known as "true north." Magnetic fields over the earth create another north, called "magnetic north," which is the only one recognizable by a magnetic compass in an airplane. The two are located several hundred miles apart, so when planning a cross-country flight, pilots must adjust course for the difference in degrees between true and magnetic north. This "magnetic variation" is displayed on aeronautical charts.

You may have noticed that handheld magnetic compasses are inaccurate when moved or bumped around. To get around that problem in airplanes, gyroscope-stabilized "heading indicators" are used to

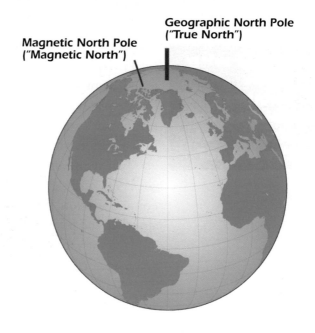

**Magnetic North Pole ("Magnetic North")**

**Geographic North Pole ("True North")**

provide stable heading information in turns, bumps, and when accelerating or decelerating. In most light airplanes, however, since the heading indicator has no magnetic sensing feature, the magnetic compass is used periodically to realign the heading indicator to north.

## 7. How do pilots fly in the clouds?

When you earn your Private Pilot certificate, you will be qualified to fly only in good weather, meaning basically when you can easily see the ground. That's because it was learned many years ago that, when trying to fly inside a cloud, even the most experienced pilot cannot comprehend the position or attitude of an airplane using only human senses.

Instrument-rated pilots are specially trained to fly using the airplane's instruments alone to determine the airplane's attitude, direction, airspeed, and position. Doing so safely requires a properly equipped plane and a good deal of intensive training. A pilot flying "IFR" (by instrument flight rules) must also master additional flight regulations, distinctive charts, and extensive and specialized radio communications with Air Traffic Control.

Once mastered, instrument flying is exciting and enjoyable, plus it greatly improves the utility of travel by light aircraft due to expanded weather capability. As you might imagine, many private pilots go on to earn instrument ratings once they're comfortable with visual flying.

## 8. Simulators for training

Not long ago, simulator training meant using a fairly simple mechanical device that resembled an airplane's controls and instrument panel. Today, simulators are extremely realistic with computer-generated displays that give you a visual perspective, as well as instrument response, all while tracking your flight path.

In the course of your flight training, you may use a flight simulator (or, in official terms, a "flight training device") at your flight school. This full-size replica of the instruments and controls of an aircraft provides you with the experience of instrument flying (flying only by reference to the instruments) without the expense of renting an airplane.

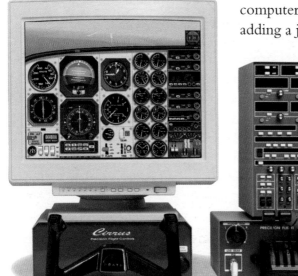

At home, you can take advantage of the computer flight simulation programs (even adding a joystick and rudder pedals) that simulate real scenarios in flying. It's just another way of learning and is useful in many ways to familiarize you with an aircraft's instruments and controls.

While the reciprocating engine (also known as a piston engine—the same kind found in your car), which powers your airplane, has some things in common with turbine (jet) engines, the two types are very different in most respects.

As you can see from the diagram, both types of engines have the same basic stages of operation: intake, compression, combustion, and exhaust. But the similarities largely end there, the biggest difference being that in a reciprocating engine those stages happen one at a time, while in a turbine engine all of them are continuous. Reciprocating aircraft engines burn gasoline, while turbine engines

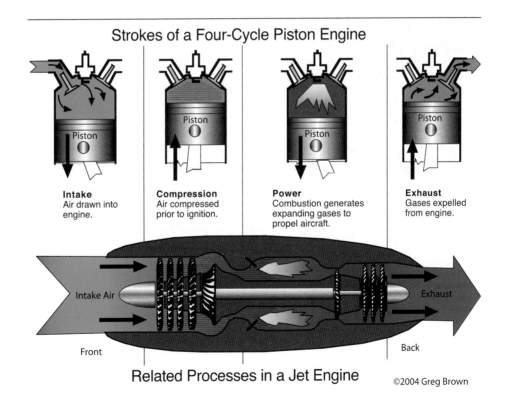

### Strokes of a Four-Cycle Piston Engine

**Intake**
Air drawn into engine.

**Compression**
Air compressed prior to ignition.

**Power**
Combustion generates expanding gases to propel aircraft.

**Exhaust**
Gases expelled from engine.

Intake Air

Exhaust

Front

Back

### Related Processes in a Jet Engine

©2004 Greg Brown

consume jet fuel, which is kerosene. Turbine engines produce a great deal more power for their weight than piston engines but are much more expensive to manufacture.

It's worth noting that, while the plane you'll fly probably has a piston engine turning a propeller to pull it through the air, turbine engines can be designed either to operate as jets, or to drive propellers themselves. A turbine engine driving a propeller is known as a turboprop.

## 10. Can airplanes fly in the rain?

Rain itself is rarely a problem for airplanes. What must be avoided are conditions where you can't see the ground due to poor visibility. Rain is rarely heavy enough to cause that problem in itself, but sometimes when it's also hazy or foggy, it's best to avoid it. It's also important to stay at least ten to twenty miles away from thunderstorms. Even with thunderstorms, however, it's not the rain that's the biggest problem but rather the turbulence within the storm cell.

Your instructor will postpone the lesson if the weather is unsafe. But if there's just some light rain in the area, she may say, "Let's go!" It's actually pretty cool to fly in the rain, providing visibility is good and there are no thunderstorms. You'll like it!

## 11. What is dewpoint? And why do pilots need to know about it?

Dewpoint is the temperature to which the air must be cooled to become completely saturated with water. So when the air temperature and the dew point are the same, you have clouds, fog, or rain (usually fog). When the temperature and dewpoint are far apart, the air is dry. When they're close together, it's very humid.

Here's what it means for pilots. Let's say you're flying just before sunset, and you hear that the temperature is only a few degrees above the dewpoint at your destination. (The dewpoint and temperature are regularly reported at most airports.) Since night is coming, the temperature will probably drop, especially if it's a clear night. If the temperature is only a few degrees above dewpoint, it may cool to the dewpoint before you get there. And then you've got fog.

Pilots know that, if the temperature and dewpoint are within four degrees of each other on a clear evening, fog may form very soon. You will want to pick a place to land before that happens.

## 12. Fueling an airplane

When you preflight the airplane before starting the engine, you will visually check the airplane's fuel and oil supply. You will determine the amount of fuel in the airplane's fuel tanks, which are usually located in the wings, by measuring the fuel with a plastic dip gauge. Training aircraft, like the one you'll likely learn in, usually have enough fuel capacity for three to four hours of flying time. Knowing how many "hours" of fuel you have in your tanks is as important as knowing how many gallons you have on board.

Part of the preflight is to drain some of the gas from the fuel tanks with a clear sample container. One reason to check the fuel is to be sure that it is free of water and contaminants. Water does not mix with gas and is heavier, so it appears as a bubble at the bottom of the container. Another reason to take a sample is to check to see that it's the right color.

Different engines use different grades of aviation fuel. To ensure that airplanes get the correct fuel grade, suppliers dye the fuels with specific colors. Most often, light aircraft use 100LL (100 low-lead), which is dyed blue; many older aircraft use 80 Octane, which is dyed red; and jets use Jet A fuel, which is clear to yellowish.

## 13. Weight & Balance

Unlike a car that you can load up as long as the trunk closes, adding passengers and baggage to an airplane requires careful thought. Too much heavy stuff in the rear baggage compartment may make it difficult to recover from a stall. Too much weight in the front may make it hard to raise the nose, or "flare," when landing. There is specific weight and balance information in every airplane's operating handbook that must be adhered to for safe and efficient flying. Your instructor will teach you to how compute an airplane's weight and balance, which is part of every pilot's planning before a flight.

## *Where Do I Go From Here?*

### Add to your flying skills with advanced flight training

Now that we've discussed in detail earning your Private Pilot certificate in airplanes, let's touch on some of the other flight training and certificates or ratings which may be earned by pilots. As you remember, the Private Pilot certificate allows you to fly in good weather for pleasure and personal business in single-engine airplanes.

Good pilots know you can never learn too much about flying. Besides, most people who love to fly want to be up in the air as much as possible. Some pilots continue to train for additional proficiency alone; others may be looking ahead to an aviation job or profession. In any case, each step on your flight path is an important one. Every lesson and different instructor adds to the bank of knowledge that makes you a better pilot. As you will see, there is a logical order to the training steps, although how and when pilots approach them varies considerably.

Any new single-engine airplane that you learn to fly requires additional training that will improve your overall flying skills. Whether it's a tailwheel airplane, a biplane, an antique warbird, or an experimental homebuilt airplane, they're all different, yet the principals of flight remain the same. Your Private Pilot certificate is your ticket to "add on" to your existing skills.

Tying down a Cessna 140 at Creston Airport, Iowa.

Why would anyone want to earn additional certificates or ratings? Many people fly for a lifetime with only a Private Pilot certificate and have a great time, never feeling the need to acquire more formal training. Others would like to be able to fly in less-than-perfect weather, or to fly more advanced airplanes like seaplanes or multi-engine aircraft. Another reason for additional training is to qualify as a professional pilot in commercial operations, like becoming a flight instructor, or carrying people and property for hire.

By now, you might be asking, "What's the difference between a certificate and a rating?" A pilot "certificate" is the basic flying license held by an aviator. There are only five types of pilot certificates: Recreational Pilot (a limited version of the Private Pilot certificate), Private Pilot, Commercial Pilot, Airline Transport Pilot, and Flight Instructor. Each defines what kinds of operations a pilot may legally participate in.

A separate issue is what sorts of aircraft a pilot may fly, and under what weather conditions. These qualifications are added as "ratings" to whatever level certificate a pilot may hold. Common pilot ratings include: instrument, single and multi-engine airplane, seaplane or helicopter.

Here are brief descriptions of some of the available pilot certificates and ratings. We'll address them in the order most pilots earn them after receiving their Private Pilot certificate.

## Instrument Rating

An Instrument rating allows pilots to fly properly equipped and certified aircraft under reduced weather conditions, like in clouds and poor visibility, under Instrument Flight Rules (IFR). This rating, while perhaps the most challenging of all pilot credentials to earn, also ranks among the most useful. With it, pilots find themselves able to use their pilot certificates under all but the worst weather conditions. Many private pilots find an IFR "ticket" invaluable, while for commercial pilots an instrument rating is virtually indispensable.

### Commercial Pilot Certificate

The Commercial Pilot certificate allows pilots to fly under a variety of "for hire" situations, including glider towing and charter flying. It is governed by additional federal training and qualification requirements, and is required for Flight Instructor applicants. Although all professional pilots must have a Commercial Pilot certificate, not all commercial pilots are professional pilots. Some pilots, after they have acquired the minimum 250 hours of flight time, take the additional training because it fine-tunes their flying skills with maximum performance maneuvers such as "lazy 8s" and "chandelles." Besides the practical and knowledge tests, additional night training and instrument training are required, as well as a minimum of ten hours of flight time in a retractable gear airplane.

### Airline Transport Pilot Certificate

The Airline Transport Pilot certificate, or "ATP," is the highest level certificate a pilot can hold. (Some call it "the Ph.D. of flying.") To earn an ATP, pilots must have at least 1,500 hours of total time as a pilot

and pass a challenging practical test fraught with simulated emergencies. An ATP certificate is required of all pilots who act as captain of scheduled commercial flights in aircraft having more than nineteen seats.

### Certificated Flight Instructor Certificate

Holders of this certificate (called CFIs) are qualified to give flight training to others. There are a few unique aspects of the Flight Instructor certificate. First, it is the only pilot certificate that must be held in conjunction with another certificate; that is, in order to be a Flight Instructor you must also hold a Commercial or Airline Transport Pilot certificate.

Also, the CFI is the only pilot certificate that carries an expiration date. Flight Instructors must renew their certificates every two years, or else lose them altogether. CFIIs are Flight Instructors with an Instrument Instructor rating, that is, they can provide instrument flight training to pilots applying for their Instrument Rating. MEIs, or Multi-engine Instructors, can give flight training in multi-engine airplanes.

## Airplane Class Ratings

A *multi-engine rating* allows pilots to operate aircraft having more than one engine. Small twin-engine airplanes fly very much like single-engine airplanes, so most of the training is spent performing simulated engine-out emergencies, or flying with only one operational engine.

If you like to be on the water, you might want to consider getting your *seaplane rating*. Many people associate seaplanes with Alaska flying, but there are many lakes in the "lower 48" and Canada that make seaplane flying a reasonable goal. Although the rating requires the necessary flight training to pass a practical test, there is no specific number of hours required.

## Aircraft Category Ratings

Many of us tend to think of what pilots do pretty narrowly—they fly airplanes, right? Certainly that assumption applies to the largest number of pilots, but there are other categories of aircraft to fly, too, and qualifying to fly them requires appropriate ratings on whatever level of pilot certificate you may hold.

Federal regulations divide these different aerial vehicles into "aircraft categories," of which airplanes are one. Pilots must hold a rating for every category they fly. The five are:

- Airplane
- Rotorcraft (Helicopter or Gyroplane)
- Glider
- Lighter-than-air (Airship or Balloon)
- Powered-lift

### Aircraft Type Ratings

A pilot must earn a "type" rating on his or her certificate for two groups of aircraft: those airplanes certified to fly at loaded weights over 12,500 pounds, and any jet, regardless of size. Type ratings are earned through a practical test for each type of aircraft flown. As you might imagine, extensive training and preparation is required for each type rating earned.

### Training always pays off

Remember that flight training at any level is *always* valuable. If you earn your instrument rating and never fly on an IFR flight plan, or if you earn your multi-engine rating and never fly a twin-engine airplane again, you will still benefit from the experience, expand your flying knowledge and become a better pilot.

Unless you're on the fast track to a career in aviation, there is no set time or order for you to advance your flight training. After you have flown a hundred hours or so on your Private Pilot certificate, the steps will become clearer to you. You'll know if and when you're ready for instrument training or your commercial certificate. Any additional training you take will improve your proficiency, which will increase your confidence and enhance your flying experience.

That's part of the beauty and reward of being a pilot; there's always something new and exciting to learn.